Exploring School Leadership in England and the Caribbean

Also available from Bloomsbury

An Intellectual History of School Leadership Practice and Research,
Helen M. Gunter
Successful School Leadership: International Perspectives, Petros Pashiardis
and Olof Johansson
Educational Leadership for a More Sustainable World, Mike Bottery
*Education in the Balance: Mapping the Global Dynamics of
School Leadership,* Raphael Wilkins
Leading Schools in Challenging Circumstances: Strategies for Success,
Philip Smith and Les Bell
Sustainable School Transformation: An Inside-Out School Led Approach,
David Crossley

Exploring School Leadership in England and the Caribbean

New Insights from a Comparative Approach

Paul Miller

Bloomsbury Academic
An imprint of Bloomsbury Publishing Plc

B L O O M S B U R Y
LONDON · OXFORD · NEW YORK · NEW DELHI · SYDNEY

Bloomsbury Academic

An imprint of Bloomsbury Publishing Plc

50 Bedford Square	1385 Broadway
London	New York
WC1B 3DP	NY 10018
UK	USA

www.bloomsbury.com

BLOOMSBURY and the Diana logo are trademarks of Bloomsbury Publishing Plc

First published 2016

British Library Cataloguing-in-Publication Data
A catalogue record for this book is available from the British Library.

ISBN: HB: 978-1-4742-5169-3
       ePDF: 978-1-4742-5171-6
       ePub: 978-1-4742-5170-9

Library of Congress Cataloging-in-Publication Data
A catalog record for this book is available from the Library of Congress.

Typeset by RefineCatch Limited, Bungay, Suffolk
Printed and bound in Great Britain

Contents

Spotlights

About the Author

Paul Miller has taught in secondary schools in Jamaica and England (London). He has provided consultancy services to schools and has also supported teachers and principals on master's and doctoral studies in education at three universities, both in Jamaica and England. He has been programme leader and research supervisor for master's and doctoral courses in education (leadership and management) in three universities, both in Jamaica and England. He is a member of Council of the British Educational Leadership Management Administration Society (BELMAS); a member of the boards of the Institute for Educational Administration & Leadership – Jamaica (IEAL-J); the Commonwealth Council for Educational Administration & Management (CCEAM), and is also an associate editor of EMAL, one of the two journals of the British Educational Leadership Management Administration Society (BELMAS), of which he is also a member. He has written and published widely in the field of school leadership with a distinctive comparative edge. His is editor of *School Leadership in the Caribbean: perceptions, practices, paradigms*. Paul currently works in the Education Department at Brunel University London, UK.

Acknowledgements

I am grateful to all those persons who have encouraged and supported me throughout the period of writing this book. Special thanks to the participants whose work/experiences provide the basis for this book and therefore the opportunity to derive new insights into the practice of school leadership. Thanks to the formal reviewers commissioned by the publisher. Your comments have been useful in helping to reshape this work. Thanks also to my informal reviewers – academics and school leaders in Jamaica and in England – who provided invaluable feedback on different drafts. I am also grateful to those who became my 'sounding boards' through regular unplanned telephone conversations, as I sought to unpack ideas and to strengthen the work. To all my family for their unwavering support, but especially Paul Miller II (age 12), who helped with some of the typing so that I would have more time to spend with him.

Introduction

Successful school leadership is central to education, development and democracy, and principals, like governments the world over, are well aware of this. Education has a major role to play in any society, in deepening economic prosperity and in increasing social mobility. For education to produce these outcomes however, effective leadership from governments, from school principals and from all other sectors of an educational system must be in place, and in sync. As suggested by former UK Schools Minister, David Miliband (2003), at different times, a government and school principals themselves may be described as either the motor of progress, or its handbrake.

There are many challenges facing education systems globally. Insufficient resourcing and financing, high staff turnover, teacher burn-out, inadequate and insufficient infrastructure and space, teacher shortage, indiscipline among students and lack of sound leadership and management, are but few of these. Paradoxically however, central to an individual's and to society's development is a strong education system. Principals, more and more, are being called to higher standards of accountability, often with no additional inputs, to drive change, to increase outcomes, to, in a sense, transform society through schooling. As education moves up the political agenda, it is being seen increasingly as the key to unlocking not only social but also economic problems (Lubienski, 2009). In countries, both in the developed and developing world, inadequate spending on education continues to challenge the ability of teachers and principals to harness the economies of scale from universal provision and use them as the foundation for a personalized service to students. It is crucial to successful teaching and leadership for teachers and principals to exercise creativity and innovation, although these may come to nothing without essential resources being in place.

This book is intended to highlight and underline the fact that the practice and enactment of school leadership is not linear and/or uni-directional; and that this fact applies to principals in both developing and developed countries. School principals across the globe juggle many tasks and roles and have found themselves vilified by parents, politicians, staff, students and other actors. The gap between what principals do versus what they are perceived to do is a real one, due, in part, to a lack of information about their work roles and judgements based on anecdotes and not facts. This is by no means to suggest that all principals are excellent or even good. Studies from around the world continue to identify poor leadership, weak leadership and ineffective leadership among principals (National Education Inspectorate, 2010; Ofsted, 2012). There are many reasons for this, some of which include changes to how principals are employed and who gets appointed as principals. For example, there is some evidence that in Jamaica and England, some principals are appointed without having previously taught in schools. This is not to suggest that all individuals appointed as a principal without a background in and experience of teaching fail or will fail, but such appointments raise questions about individual and school effectiveness that should not be ignored.

The factors underpinning a principal's success or failure are multiple and range from personal, social, cultural and legal to religious and institutional. These factors provide qualitatively different points of reference for understanding professional practice, compared with traditional sets of assumptions that have hitherto guided our understanding of school leadership practice. And it is perhaps these factors that contribute to a challenge being experienced globally to recruiting high quality, experienced principals. Indeed, not only do these factors help to determine school leadership practice, they are sometimes responsible for creating tensions within this practice. As illustrated by Grace (1995) and Earley et al. (2012), local management of schools and rapid changes in educational policy has led to the intensification of work by principals. In Grace's view, 'the culture of individual school leadership, as practised by the individual headteacher is breaking' (p. 203), which, according to Gronn (2003, p. 2) has 'resulted in a reliance on distributed forms of leadership practices in schools'. Nevertheless, as distributed practices appear to become routinized, governments are introducing and strengthening existing leadership accountability measures and systems, such as, for example, the Office for Standards in Education (Ofsted) in England and the National Educational Inspectorate (NEI) in Jamaica; although, in Gronn's view, such institutions exacerbate work intensification.

Wenger's (1991, p. 229) observation that 'one can design roles, but one cannot design the identities that will be constructed through those roles' renders the work of the National College for Teaching and Leadership in England and the National College for Educational Leadership in Jamaica somewhat problematic. That is, there are limits to what a training college and a training programme can do to create the kinds of principals that will raise the bar of performance for schools in a climate of increased performance expectations. No two principals are alike. Indeed, no two individuals are alike. Yet, a common trend among political actors is a 'one-size-fits-all' approach to training, supported by a blanketized view of accountability and blame. Torrington and Weightman (1989) suggested that 'extraordinary centrality' and 'almost universal focus' on a principal's job is evidenced 'in the continuing statements of politicians' (p. 135). Tyack and Cuban (1995, p. 14), caution that those responsible for schools need to be careful, since education and actors in schools can easily shift 'from panacea to scapegoat'. Menter et al. (1995, p. 311) talk of the principal having to 'carry the can'; similarly Jones (1987, p. 152) points out that 'sometimes the head is the Aunt Sally, a scapegoat'.

The impact of what seems like unrelenting changes and exacting measures of accountability is likely to impact each principal in different ways, given the location and size of a school, the qualifications and experience of staff, the gender make-up of the student body and the support and/or challenge received from both the parents and the school board. It is arguable that, while some principals and staff will feel powerless in the face of growing external constraints, others will show creativity and resilience, improvising or making do, in every area of their practice, using what Suchman called 'workarounds' (1995, p. 575). In other words, in as much as the pace of change and the measures of accountability can constrain practice, to an extent, they also provide opportunities for a principal to show spontaneity, creativity and ingenuity.

Until just over two decades ago, much of literature and research on school leadership in England was through small-scale case studies (Hall & Southworth, 1997 (published online 25 August 2010). However, PricewaterhouseCoopers LLP (2007), Earley et al. (2012) and Matthews et al. (2014) provide a rich source of data and analysis on school leadership and school leadership practices in England through different lenses and covering a range of issues. In Jamaica, research into school leadership is a relatively new phenomenon, punctuated by a number of recent small-scale national studies (Hutton, 2011; Miller 2012, 2013a, 2013b, 2013c, 2014). Nevertheless, research into school leadership has tended to only partially reflect the realities and experiences of school principals (Hughes, 1976) leading Ball (1987) to suggest that 'There is a general failure to come to grips with the "street realities" of headship' (p. 8). What is missing from the existing literature are actual accounts of principals in different country contexts concerning the nitty gritty of their jobs, underscoring Blasé and Anderson's (1995, p. 25) assertion that the data which needs to be collected on school leadership should encompass the 'little stuff of everyday life', compare and contrast practice and integrate debates about issues, thereby contributing to new conceptual insights. The accounts of principals in this book are drawn from two different world communities, providing new insights into school leadership practices related to the nitty gritty and street realities of a principal's work and role.

As far back as 1993, Southworth called for this kind of analysis into principals' work roles, suggesting, 'given our relatively meagre understanding of leadership, not only do we need more descriptions of leaders in action, we also need richer and detailed descriptions of them at work ... Until we expand our knowledge ... our understanding of how they lead will remain simplistic and superficial' (1993, p. 79). His points were elaborated by Bolman and Heller (1995) in their view that much of the literature on leadership is irrelevant to school leaders as it is '... too abstract and detached from practice or too narrow and disengaged from person and context, and therefore, of little use to those in schools' (p. 342).

Methodology

There have been a number of calls for a new paradigm of research in educational leadership, at a time when educational leadership and management has gained increased prominence and attention. Using an approach that incorporates aspects of grounded theory, ethnomethodology and conversational analysis, this book presents an integrated study of the practice of school leadership from the perspective of 10 principals: four from Jamaica and six from England. Grounded theory was developed by Glaser and Strauss (1976), its main aim to generate theories and insights regarding social phenomena. That is, to develop understanding not based on *a priori* assumptions but instead that is 'grounded' in, or derived from, a thorough data analysis. Thus, for Glaser and Strauss, 'generating grounded theory is a way of arriving at theory suited to its supposed uses' (p. 3).

According to Atkinson and Heritage (1984), ethnomethodology is a method for understanding the social orders people use to make sense of the world through analysing their accounts and descriptions of their day-to-day experiences. As a methodology, ethnomethodology seeks to find the methods used by 'actors in everyday interaction which achieve the sense of order in their contexts'. Ethnomethodology focuses on the achievement of a sense of order through the actions of participants and does not seek to explore macro patterns of social 'structure' – rather, how these patterns impact them. In other words, in presenting the cases in the way I have, I have kept in mind the need to 'enable heads to speak for themselves' (Mortimore & Mortimore, 1991, p. vii).

Conversation analysis emerged out of the ethnomethodological challenge to mainstream research methods. Over time, conversational analysis has gained prominence and can no longer be viewed as an untested approach (Rayner & Ribbins, 1999). Ribbins and Marland (1994) suggest that conversational analysis helps to position the role of principals and research into school leadership firstly, as a situated perspective that gives full access to the views and actions of principals across a range of events and issues; and secondly, as a contextualized perspective in action which examines what principals say in the context of what they do (p. 6).

Data-gathering for this book involved several, mostly informal, face-to-face, one-to-one conversations with school principals, occurring over a period of five years, between 2009 and 2014. In choosing this approach, it was believed it would provide readers with a sense of individuality through portrait-based accounts told by each principal. Given the book has emerged from conversations with principals during my work with them, I should point out that it was never my intention to attempt to offer a representative sample. I am however grateful that the principals are from primary and secondary schools, at different points in their careers as principals, are males and females, have different background and life experiences, and within their respective countries are from relatively different physical locations.

Participants

There are 10 principals, seven females and three males. All four Jamaican principals are females whereas there are three males and three female principals from England. Together the 10 principals have a combined 163 years of teaching experience or an average of 16.3 years individually. Jamaican principals have a combined 62 years' teaching experience or an individual average of 15.5 years. English principals have a combined 101 years' teaching experience or an individual average of 16.8 years.

There are five primary school principals and five secondary school principals. Three principals lead schools in inner-city communities; four in urban/suburban areas and three in rural/remote areas. All four Jamaican principals have experience of being a principal in only one school whereas all English principals have experience of being a principal in between two and three schools.

The average age among the 10 principals is 44.1 years. Two had been in post for five years; two for eight years; four for one year; one for six years and one for two years. Together the principals have a total of 38 years of current leadership experience. The four Jamaican principals have 22 years of combined *current* leadership experience or an individual average of 5.5. English principals have a total of 16 years of combined *current* leadership experience or an individual average of 2.6 years. For *overall* leadership experience, Jamaican principals have a combined 23 years, whereas English principals have a combined 52 years.

Structure of book

This book places the views and experiences of principals at the heart of the debate and discussion about their practice through a form of conversational analysis. It provides insights into and understandings of the behind-the-scenes happenings in the world and work of principals, highlighting the conflictful nature of decision-making and the challenges they encounter in trying to comply with policy and contextual practicalities. The book does not only give voice and agency to principals, it also allows them their personality as individuals, so easily hidden behind their titles and based on society's construction of them. The book also provides a close-up view of the nature and context of school leadership from multiple settings and multiple locations in two very different countries: culturally, economically, technologically, socially, geopolitically and in terms of their education systems. The book also presents examples and accounts of school leadership that bring to life the reality that the practice of school leadership is messy and chaotic; is both evolutionary and revolutionary; is culturally, socially and contextually situated; and is legally situated but individually experienced and practised. In other words, the book presents and represents a 'melting pot' of evidence, experiences and ideas about the practice of school leadership in a single volume accessible to school leaders in different world communities and communities of practice.

The book has the following eight chapters: Chapter 1, 'The Changing Nature of School Leadership'; Chapter 2, 'Curricular and Instructional Leadership'; Chapter 3, 'Diversity Leadership'; Chapter 4, 'Technology Leadership'; Chapter 5, 'Policy Leadership'; Chapter 6, 'People Leadership'; Chapter 7, 'Entrepreneurial and Safety Leadership'; and Chapter 8, 'Evaluation, Implications and Conclusions'.

1

The Changing Nature of School Leadership

As more countries require better achievement from their schools and grant greater autonomy to schools in designing curricula and managing resources, the role of the school leader has grown far beyond that of administrator...

Schleicher, 2012, p. 20

Much less is being spent on education in real terms by many governments, when more is being demanded; fewer teachers are being employed at a time when some systems are experiencing growth in pupil numbers and class sizes; and education institutions are struggling to respond in a timely manner to changes in their environment brought about by the impact of information and communications technology. That said, educational leadership in these unpredictable and swiftly changing times requires an approach that is neither top-down nor bottom-up, but that is encompassing, synergistic, innovative, and practical.

Miller, 2012, p. 9

Introduction

School leadership is not a unitary exercise. Nor is it a linear exercise. School leadership is as dynamic and as spontaneous as the environment within which it is practised, mediated through a range of factors including cultural, social, economic, legal, technological and personal. Some of these factors may be further classified as internal or external. The range of factors and subdivisions are arguably infinite, increasing each month, each year, with a change in government and in line with global events. Yet, it is these factors, working together and/or against each other, that explain how a principal constructs and applies leadership.

Faced with cultural, social, economic, national and sometimes international policy directives – for example, improvements in the performance of students played out in what I call the 'court of accountability' through the lever of national inspectorates – education ministries and/or departments generally and school principals in particular are forced to 'do education differently' (Miller, 2012, p. 9). This doing of education differently is not only to be noticed in how school principals lead and teachers teach, but there are also noticeable differences in the types of policies pursued by governments; in how the policies are pursued; in the ways governments communicate with and monitor schools; in the ways principals communicate with parents; and in the way principals monitor teaching and learning and generally what goes on at school. The recent economic meltdown, coupled with advances in technology, globalization and changes to the borderland narrative have also had an impact on the ability of schools to deliver successful quality education and as a result have had an impact on the ability of some principals to deliver dynamic and effective school leadership (Harris & Mixon, 2014).

Workload

The work of school principals has, and continues to, become more complex and challenging, creating what Grace (1995) described as 'principals' work intensification' (p. 203). Intensification of work is largely a feature of challenges in the external environment of schools, such as bureaucracy, which in turn fuel and heighten internal challenges – for example, around issues such as procurement, budgeting and staff recruitment, leading to excessive paperwork. As Earley et al. (2012) note, 'In the United Kingdom ... following Local Management of Schools reform from the late 1980s, schools were seen to have become more complex to manage especially in terms of budgets, human resources, professional development and administration' (p. 21).

Using data from a range of sources, PricewaterhouseCoopers (PwC) (2007) reported that a number of school principals had difficulty achieving a work-life balance due to the long hours they work. Although PwC reported that some school leaders did not prioritize and some did not delegate, the study linked the inability of some to achieve a work-life balance with the number of hours they had to work to get the job done and the number of tasks they had to complete. The PwC study categorized the responsibilities of principals into six main areas: accountability; strategy and improvement planning; managing teaching and learning; managing staffing (recruitment and development); networking with other institutions; and day to-day operations, all of which require lots of time from principals, which can sometimes get in the way of strategic visioning. The relevance of these six areas will become clearer throughout the book.

Policy reforms

There are several events currently happening globally that impact the successful practice of school leadership. The creation of education markets, for example, is impacting, sometimes negatively, on school principals and has nearly always been at the expense of their own professional development and training. Further, reforms in education, globally, have led to the introduction of high-stakes accountability measures such as standards-based testing and the monitoring of schools through inspections. School inspections have now become routine in small and large countries, in developed and developing countries, with an aim, arguably, of pointing fingers at failing schools, but also to establish the impact of schools on pupils and communities. As competition within and between schools in a country intensifies, competition between schools in several countries has intensified as policy-makers, education ministry officials and school principals try to climb higher in the relevant league tables. This has resulted in a culture of performativity, characterized by a focus on outcomes, leading Stevens et al. (2005) to suggest that increased accountability measures and administrative demands demotivate rather than encourage school principals.

With improvement through standards and control, the emphasis appears to be on standards, not structures and not creativity. Governments' control over education has been increased and is reinforced, more and more, by punitive measures – for example, through the increasing use of compulsory testing, targets, centralized school control, control of the teacher training curriculum, surveillance and monitoring of those involved in teacher education and training, and the punishment of 'failing' teachers, schools, educational authorities and those involved in teacher training. One could therefore argue that the focus of school improvement is on managerialism and not creativity, secured through educational policies which focus on improving school performance and not on improving schools, and also through the blaming and shaming of teachers and principals. This is currently a global phenomenon in education.

Social justice

In recent years, a market culture that privileges competition and consumerism has steadily crept into the field of education. At the base of this market culture is capitalism, which is concerned with the production and trade of goods and/or services based on private ownership of wealth, competition, free buying and selling, and limited government interference. A fundamental problem of this market culture in education is that capitalist systems are known to increase the gap between rich and poor, thereby making the idea of equality between peoples less likely (Sage, 2014). This presents a dilemma for schools, which promote equality of opportunity and inclusive practices as essential principles underpinning learning in a diverse society, and for principals, whose student population is made up of many – or mostly – poor students. Put differently, the market culture in education, underpinned by recent events in the global economy, has led to many new poor students, many additional poor students and students shunning school due to being unable to pay fees or due to their inability to pay for lunch, transportation, material and equipment.

Wilkinson and Picket (2009) condemn the widening gap between rich and poor, calling for a dismantling of the current market system of 'the winner takes all'. Stiglitz (2012) sustains this view by arguing that inequality demotivates and depresses the oppressed. Picketty (2014) scoffs at the idea that hard work and academic success will produce monetary benefits for individuals and families; while Negus (2014) suggests that modern (state) education exacerbates inequality. These views represent a challenge to those involved in education – in schools, colleges and universities – who teach and who are also led to believe that diligence and good grades will lead to social mobility in the form of well paid jobs and a reasonable standard of living. In England and in Jamaica, for example, the increasing costs of higher education has had an impact on those entering university, and therefore on the aspirations of those most in need. The gap between rich and poor has therefore been widened rather than narrowed, and a school is a prime site for where such gaps are played out.

Multiculturalism

Multiculturalism in education has received considerable attention in recent years (Race & Lander, 2014; Smith, 2012). Regarded as problematic, several high profile publications have debated how multiculturalism can impact, both directly and indirectly, on how principals do their jobs, whether in developing countries (Craig, 2002; UNESCO, 1995) or developed countries (Troyna & Hatcher, 1992). Multiculturalism in education in England, for example, has been viewed with scepticism and suspicion and has been described as 'an irredeemably deracialized' discourse of schooling, and an 'educational approach which reifie[s] culture and cultural difference' (Modood & May, 2001, p. 308). I will return to these issues in Chapter 3.

Gender

The right of girls to education is being recognized with a gradual dismantling of religious and other cultural strictures that have, so far, led to or aided their exclusion from mainstream schooling. Simultaneously, changes to educational structures through, for example, initiatives such as the Millennium Development Goals (MDGs), have increased the participation of children in education and of girls in particular, although national policy responses and resources at the school level are not always in place to support improvement and/or sustain demand (United Nations, 2010). In Jamaica and England, the participation of children in education, especially at the primary level, is broadly in line with the MDGs 2015 benchmark figure, although in both countries boys' achievement continues to be an area of concern. How principals seek to address and respond to participation and achievement will be discussed further in Chapter 3.

Inclusion

Inclusion is contested within and across educational systems and in theory and practice in the countries of the North and of the South (Armstrong et al., 2011) and as a result, the meaning of inclusion is framed by different national and international contexts. Nevertheless, the education of children and young people with special educational needs and physical disabilities has been spotlighted in international forums such as the United Nations, resulting in the passage and enactment of laws and policies, respectively, as national governments and institutions try to bring about changes to discourses of deficit and associated practices in several countries. The implications for schools and their leaders are clear. Further, the educational rights of traveller children (Wilkin et al., 2010), indigenous children (UNICEF/Innocenti Research Centre, 2004), migrants and refugees (Arnot & Gelsthorpe, 2010; Shotte, 2003) have also received international attention with some countries making concerted efforts to revise policy and practice so that, to the extent that it is possible, children and young people from these communities can seamlessly participate in mainstream schooling (United Nations, 2011). These areas of progress reflect, simultaneously, sites of challenge, not least for school principals, but also for entire school communities.

Technology

The use and impacts of digital and information communication technologies (ICTs) in education has become a matter of challenge and priority for school principals (Grady, 2011b). Technology leadership emphasizes that leaders should develop, guide, manage and apply technology to different organizational operations in order to improve operational performance. Technology leadership is therefore a functionally oriented leadership practice (Chin, 2010). The advancement, application and potential of technology has infused new energy into educational reform, with many countries acknowledging that sound technology leadership is or will become an important strategy for improving academic quality and student achievement (Means & Olson, 1995; Ullman, 2013). The implications for a school principal are clear. However, whereas some schools have an adequate ICT infrastructure and the provision of ICT is embedded into teaching and learning, others are the opposite. Similarly, whereas some principals lack the relevant skills in ICT to simplify their work, thereby allowing them to achieve a better work-life balance, others use technology to improve professional and personal efficiency. In addition, some principals try to bridge the digital gap that exists between teachers and students whereas others do not always make this a priority (International Society for Technology in Education, 2008).

Economic environment

As pointed out earlier, recent and ongoing changes in the global economic environment have meant a reduction in most national budgetary allocations to education (Leachman & Mai, 2014). The result has been schools and other educational institutions in both developed and developing countries can sometimes struggle to fund essential activities. In a number of developing countries, teachers' monthly salary payments have also been delayed, sometimes for weeks at a time. In other cases, many schools have entered into 'cost-sharing' arrangements directly with government or through other schemes with private sector entities. In the main, budgetary cuts to spending on education have meant a reduction or loss of essential services or the curtailment of some provision. Ahead of the global financial crisis, the UK's former Schools Minister, David Miliband, summed up the existing financial challenges facing schools in England in a speech to principals:

> There is no easy answer in a complex system. And to work, any system is going to require head[teachers] to rise to the challenge of effective budget management.

In last week's Ofsted report one quarter of secondary schools struggled to support educational priorities through financial planning, and 40% struggled with appraisal and performance management. Both have implications for the budget. I understand and want to reflect upon and respond to your desire for longer term, simpler mechanisms for financial planning. But I need your help on a number of fronts: to squeeze out relatively unproductive costs, whether on cover for absence or energy costs; and to recognise that in any organisation where 80% plus of the spend is on people, decisions on pay and promotion are critical to budgetary discipline; the more we pay existing staff the less we have for extra staff, which is a key element in our joint priority of workload reduction. We in government have a duty to help – with early information and better coordination with LEAs. But you can make the difference between success and failure.

                                                                                    Miliband, 2003

These observations are still as pertinent today as they were back in 2003. In both Jamaica and the United Kingdom, teachers, like other public sector employees, have had to agree to pay freezes delivered through austerity (United Kingdom) and structural adjustment (Jamaica) mechanisms, as national governments try to rebalance national budgets and lift their economies out of recession. In Jamaica for example, in 2013 the majority of public sector workers, including teachers, and their unions, signed a wage freeze agreement until 2016 as part of the conditions for an International Monetary Fund (IMF) loan. At the moment, there are ongoing debates about the possibility of extending the wage freeze to 2017. Similarly, in 2010, the United Kingdom's Conservative-led Coalition Government introduced the most dramatic budget cuts in living memory, outstripping measures taken by other advanced economies which are also under pressure to reduce public spending and debt. The measures were set to end in 2016, although in 2014 the government decided that a 2018 end to current austerity measures was more realistic. It is suspected that similar cut-backs and concessions are being demanded by governments of educational systems across the world. In Jamaica, for example, national budgetary allocations to education were already in decline for up to a decade before the introduction of recent structural adjustment measures (Johnston & Montecino, 2012).

The context of leadership

As we have come to realize, schools are operating in a rapidly changing context. This rapidly changing context – economic, social, technological, social, legal and political – is compounded by complexity and uncertainty at all levels of society. Schools and other educational institutions are changing in paradoxical ways – on the one hand, becoming more complex, more different, more similar, more intricately connected both internally and externally, and on the other becoming more lonely and more isolated from their publics. According to Merry (1995), humankind appears to be in the midst of a chaotic transformation on various fronts.

The volatility of the *environment* is pushing individuals to be more resilient, more flexible, more adaptable. Having adapted to one change, another is forced upon individuals, bringing more complexity and uncertainty. The challenge is for principals to operate under rapidly mutating circumstances, which requires a rethink of paradigms of leadership in theory and in practice. In other words, as school principals around the world continue to adapt and respond to changes in a school's external environment, different models of leadership are engaged (indeed are required!) in order to lead successful and effective schools.

Between families of schools, or between schools in a region and/or education zone, systems leadership is being engaged and experimented with more and more (Hill & Matthews, 2010), and within schools distributed leadership has been gathering pace (Harris & Spillane, 2008). These developments are important for two clear reasons. First, as the policy landscape continues to experience rapid changes, nationally and internationally, schools that are serious about their progress will become involved in partnership working rather than attempting to go it alone. Second, by sharing the burden of leadership through task distribution and delegation, school leaders simultaneously 'upbuild' and 'upskill' others, reducing the time it takes to complete a task, thereby adding and unearthing new voices, capacities, skills and talents. Despite their appeal however, and despite their potential impacts, it does appear there is some way to go before distributed and systems leadership are embedded into the 'common' practice of schools and schooling.

Leader(ship) effectiveness

Boal and Hooijberg (2001) suggest the ability of leaders to effectively impact organizational performance is partly dependent on individual factors, such as a person's ability to deal with mental and behavioural complexity and social skills. They link organizational performance to visionary leadership and leader competencies such as cognitive complexity and social intelligence, arguing that individual leader capabilities, such as possessing managerial wisdom, and the capacity to change and learn, are foundational to achieving organizational effectiveness. In an attempt to understand leadership, researchers have provided different frames of reference, for example by focusing on singular aspects such as decision-making or on more integrative and holistic approaches that align leaders' and followers' ideas about leadership (Drath, 2001). On the one hand, if an individual believes that leadership is about leaders telling followers what to do, then a participative approach in which followers are consulted and expected to make decisions may be viewed as problematic. On the other hand, if an individual believes that leadership is concerned with enticing people to follow grand ideas or visions, using coercion to get people to comply, this approach too may be viewed as problematic.

Among both practitioners and researchers, leadership has been assigned an idealistic, lofty status and significance, focused around heroic individuals (Avery, 2005). This has led to some approaches, for example, transactional leadership, being pushed aside, at least in the literature, in favour of transformational leadership, which presents leaders with almost entirely positive attributes, compared with transactional leaders who tend to be accorded negative characteristics (Dunphy & Stace, 1988). A further limitation to arriving at a clear sense of leader(ship) effectiveness is underpinned by researchers and practitioners who propose that leadership is more about the followers than about leaders and their characteristics (Avery, 2005). That is, leadership is the process of being perceived by others to be a leader (den Hartog et al., 1999). In other words, leadership involves behaviours, traits, characteristics and outcomes produced by leaders as these elements are interpreted by followers (Nadler & Tuschman, 1990). Based on this view, effective leader(ship) is interwoven with follower perceptions.

Leadership has also been viewed as unnecessary and overly romanticized. Those who support this view have gone as far as proposing not using the term leadership at all (Atwater & Bass, 1994). The central role given to leadership in organizational effectiveness, some would say, makes such a criticism justified, although others would argue that such a criticism is unjustified since simply eliminating notions of leadership would leave people without a term to describe the factor that provides direction and cohesion to a group (Avery, 2005). This book focuses on revealing school leadership in its complexity, rather than abandoning the concept, and in doing so it takes a broad view of leadership, ranging from the individual, to the interpersonal, to the institutional and beyond. This is done in the context of a principal's daily work that can neither be prescribed nor contained – but is rather emergent, evolving, spontaneous dynamic and integrative.

School leadership in context

In some countries, and in some communities within some countries, social upheaval more broadly and community uprisings more locally, has hampered the effective delivery of schooling, which sometimes puts the lives of entire school communities at risk. The result of such upheavals and uprisings is the closure of schools, resulting in the loss of essential curriculum time (UNICEF, 2005). There has also been an increase in accidents and natural disasters and hazards, adversely affecting schooling and the delivery of education in both developed and developing countries, forcing schools to close and/or forcing them to adopt creative and sometimes unconventional ways of 'doing education' (Shotte, 2013), and as a result placing the matter of how principals lead at the centre of ongoing debates about their leadership. As suggested by Miller (2012), 'school leadership in times that are unpredictable and swiftly changing requires an approach that is neither top down nor bottom up but one that is encompassing, synergistic, innovative and practical' (p. 9). I will return to this idea later. Suffice to say here, however, that demands placed on principals and their leadership come at a time when, more and more, school leaders are being called upon to carefully balance intuition against logic; the intrinsic against the external; the legal against the moral; the natural against the supernatural – in order to negotiate and secure best outcomes for all who study and work in their schools.

Sound leadership and management for successful schooling is well recognized and effective leadership is the bedrock of a successful school organization (Bush, 2003). Although the stories of principals in this book are drawn from the primary and secondary phases of education only, it is still important to point out that, from nursery to university, effective leadership is leadership that is innovative, creative, responsive to changes in the environment, responsive to the needs of the client, supportive of staff and clients and visionary in outlook. As proposed by Miller (2012), 'If sound leadership at the policy level is a seed of development, then sound leadership at the levels of schools and classrooms is arguably a flower of development' (p. 9). Achieving this development is not a linear act, in that the practice of school leadership is not black and white.

School leadership practice has changed and continues to change as schools change and as the environment within which schools operate continues to change. As the demands placed on schools and the demographics around them change, the practice of school leadership will continue to occupy a prominent place in the relevant literature due to concerted interest among researchers and politicians in changing lives and solving problems to promote development both nationally and internationally. Through an integrated approach, while highlighting country characteristics as appropriate, this book sheds light on the nature of school leadership practices in two different countries, contexts, cultures and circumstances. A number of 'Spotlights' are used to articulate a range of individual, systemic, cultural, economic, social, technological, pedagogical as well as leadership practice differences and similarities.

Spotlight 1: Education in England and Jamaica

England

There are approximately 23,330 state-funded schools in England: 3,446 state secondary schools and 16,884 state primary schools. In January 2012, there were just over 7 million pupils attending state-funded primary schools, state-funded secondary schools, special schools and pupil referral units. There are approximately 451,000 teachers in the state sector in England, including just over 23,000 principals.

Educational policy reforms in England have intensified since the Conservative-led coalition government came to office in 2010. For example, there have been changes to the design and delivery of initial teacher education, changes to the secondary curriculum and massive changes to the structure and organization of schooling, most notably through the introduction of academies and free schools.

Education in England is overseen by the Department for Education (DfE) and the Department for Business, Innovation and Skills, supported by 152 local authorities (LAs). The education system is divided into early years (ages 3–4), primary education (ages 4–11), secondary education (ages 11–18) and tertiary education (ages 18+). Education is free to students in the public education system until they reach university.

Full-time education is compulsory for all children aged between 5 and 16. State-provided schooling and sixth-form education is paid for by taxes. From 1998 to the present, there have been six main types of maintained school in England: community schools, foundation and trust schools, voluntary-aided schools, voluntary-controlled schools, academies and free schools.

Jamaica

In Jamaica, there are just under 1,200 state-funded schools: 206 state-funded secondary schools and technical high schools, and 973 pre-primary, primary, all-age and junior high schools. In 2012, the education system catered to about 800,000 students in public institutions at the early childhood, primary and secondary levels. There are approximately 25,000 teachers in the state-funded sector, including just under 1,200 principals.

Over the last decade, Jamaica's education system has introduced several reforms. For example, recommendations in the Report of the Task Force on Educational Reform (2005) led to the establishment of a National College for Educational Leadership, a National Education Inspectorate, a National Council on Education, the Jamaica Teaching Council and the Jamaica Tertiary Education Commission. The Education System Transformation Programme was followed, in 2010, by the Education Sector Plan of 'Vision 2030: National Development Plan Jamaica', an ambitious multifaceted programme of activities and initiatives aimed at charting Jamaica's path to 'developed' country status by the year 2030.

Education in Jamaica is administered primarily by the Ministry of Education (MoE), through its head office and six regional offices. Formal education is provided mainly by the government, solely or in partnership with churches and trusts. Formal education also is provided by private schools. As stipulated in the 1980 Education Act, the education system consists of four levels: early childhood, primary, secondary and tertiary. There is a cost-sharing mechanism in place in Jamaica to fund education which is not free to students.

Conceptualizing leadership

If we consider the notions and suggestions about leadership, it could be argued that leadership is an essential ingredient in the effectiveness of a school. Indeed, it has been argued for generations that leadership is an important factor in the success of an institution or venture. The concept of leadership is not new and evidence of practice can be traced back to earlier periods of civilization. According to Bass (1981), the study of leadership is an ancient art and a practice that 'occurs universally among all people regardless of culture, whether they are isolated Indian villagers, Eurasian steppe nomads, or Polynesian fisher folk' (p. 5).

The field of leadership could be described as a 'mushrooming industry' where existing theories are contested, tried and denounced regularly and where others are introduced at pace. As a result, it is possible there are as many different definitions of leadership as there are persons who've tried to define the concept. Bass (1981) defined leadership as a process and a set of actions. Stogdill (1950) defined leadership as the 'process (act) of influencing' (p. 3) and later as 'initiation and maintenance of structure in expectation and interaction' (1974, p. 411). Hemphill and Coons (1957) defined leadership as 'the behavior of an individual when he is directing the activities of a group toward a shared goal' (p. 7). Regardless of the theory or definition adopted, leadership has been intimately linked to the effective functioning of institutions throughout the centuries.

The contested and fragmented nature of leadership as a field of enquiry has resulted in a challenge in defining who leaders are and what they are expected to do. Hosking (1988) suggests, '. . . leaders are those who consistently make effective contributions to social order, and who are expected and perceived to do so' (p. 153). Conger (1992) extends this view by proposing that '. . . leaders are individuals who establish direction for a working group of individuals who gain commitment from this group of members to this direction and who then motivate these members to achieve the direction's outcomes' (p. 18). In both cases, the leader is expected to shape or contribute to the shaping of 'direction', although the subjective nature of what a leader is supposed to do adds very little to our understanding of the matter at hand.

The notions and beliefs about leadership in other organizations are no different from those regarding leadership in schools. Leadership is therefore arguably the most important ingredient in the successful functioning of a school, either as a whole or as a combination of different parts. For example, Marzano et al. (2005) link the following characteristics of school leadership to the available literature:

- school mission and goals;
- climate of a school and individual classrooms;
- attitudes of teachers;
- classroom practices of teachers;
- how a curriculum is organized;
- opportunities created for students to learn;
- development and capacity-building among staff.

Given the obvious importance of leadership, it is perhaps understandable that an effective principal is thought to be a necessary prerequisite for an effective school. A 1977 US Senate Committee Report on equal educational opportunity (US Congress, 1970, p. 56) suggested the principal is the single most influential person in a school:

In many ways the school principal is the most important and influential individual in any school. He or she is the person responsible for all activities that occur in and around the school building. It is the principal's leadership that sets the tone of the school, the climate for teaching, the level of professionalism and morale of teachers, and the degree of concern for what students may or may not become. The principal is the main link between the community and the school, and the way he or she performs in this capacity largely determines the attitudes of parents and students about the school. If a school is a vibrant, innovative, child-centered place, if it has a reputation for excellence in teaching, if students are performing to the best of their ability, one can almost always point to the principal's leadership as the key to success.

The perceived importance of leadership in schools and the crucial role played by a principal in that leadership cannot be mistaken, and could lead one to think that suggestions regarding leadership practice in schools derive from much more extensive research in the field of educational/school leadership, spanning generations. School leadership, over time, has evolved into an art, a science and a process that simultaneously enlists and guides the talents and energies of staff, students and parents towards the achievement of some common educational goals. Two key elements – direction and influence – are to be noted in this definition, simultaneously underlining the act of leadership (leading) and the actions of leaders (providing leadership). While it has been relatively easy to arrive at a more widely 'accepted' definition of school leadership, the contested notions of leadership and leaders are to be seen, in the definition of school leadership itself, in relation to what school leaders do and what it is believed they should do, making its conceptualization and practice similarly contested. Having resolved that issue, let's now turn to the book's main argument.

2

Curricula and Instructional Leadership

To date, we have not found a single documented case of a school improving its student achievement record in the absence of talented leadership.

Leithwood & Seashore-Louis, 2012, p. 3

From nurseries to institutions of higher education, leadership that is innovative and creative; that is responsive to changes in the environment and to the needs of the client; that is supportive of staff and students; and that is visionary in outlook, is required to lead institutions towards their goals and towards better outcomes for all who work and study in them. Put simply, if sound leadership at the policy level is a seed of development, then sound leadership of educational institutions and at the classroom level is arguably a flower of development.

Miller, 2012, p. 9

Introduction

Principals spend considerable amounts of time investing in strategies and approaches aimed at enhancing and supporting the quality of teaching provided by teachers, and therefore the quality of learning for students. This is a fundamental role of a principal since, at the heart of a school are its learning and teaching activities. Principals also spend a lot of time being concerned with and worrying about the quality and success of their schools, the performance of students in core subjects, the performance of different groups of students, the quality, numbers and appropriate balance of staff and the school's physical infrastructure and resources. Some principals are kept awake at nights due to the threat of lawsuits; others for fear of losing their jobs and due to a school's position in national league tables; and still others, due to several other issues not so easily captured here, but which have a direct impact on teaching and learning and what goes on in a school.

The fears experienced by school principals, arguably, derive from two main sources: duty and accountability. First, principals have an obligation to students and their families to provide them with a good education that equips them with tools and skills for both now and in the future. Curricula leadership is dynamic in nature and requires a principal to regularly review a school's subject offerings to students, in line with environmental changes, the changing demands of students and new and different skills and areas of interest brought to a school by new teachers. In other words, effective curricula leadership is not accepting but moving beyond minimum standards (Goodlad, 2004). Second, a principal has internal accountability (Carnoy et al., 2003) to several internal and external stakeholders including students, teachers, the school board and parents. As a result, decisions about classroom observations and ensuring teachers assess students' work and provide adequate and thorough feedback are examples of important internal accountability approaches directly related to a school's overall performance.

The quality of instruction teachers provide underpins the academic outcomes and examination results of students and schools. Although, over time, a principal's role has shifted from mostly teaching or some teaching to less teaching or no teaching, it is the view of Coulson (1976) that the title head*teacher* confers upon the holder of such a title a special responsibility to serve and to lead learning. Put differently, a principal is arguably a master teacher, a teacher of teachers, a leader of learning first and foremost, rather than an administrator. It is this title and the freedom that comes from being in such a position of authority and influence that Coulson argues give principals the latitude to set the academic direction of their schools. In other words, principals are persons who, by word and/or personal example, should markedly influence the behaviours, thoughts and/or attitudes of teachers, and in this case, strive to to achieve instructional mastery. As suggested by Rowe and Guerrero (2013), leaders influence followers both directly and indirectly. Direct influence of their effectiveness is believed to be achieved through how they relate to others and how they embody the story they tell or the message they give. An assumption here is that principals as (instructional) leaders (should) serve as an example for motivating and inspiring others.

Nevertheless, the administrative roles performed by principals are arguably aimed at providing students with the best educational experience and also at ensuring they achieve the best outcomes from their performance in national tests. Rimmer's (2013) four-dimensional construct of instructional leadership provides some useful insights into some essential administrative duties and processes that contribute to successful teaching and learning.

- **Vision, mission and culture-building.** Principals promote a school's vision, mission and culture that focuses on learning for both students and staff, and that measures learning by improvement in instruction and in the quality of student learning.
- **Allocation of resources.** The principal, as the leader of learning, tries to ensure adequate and appropriate resources are available and that they are suited to the cultural, linguistic, physical, socioeconomic and learning needs of a school community.
- **Improvements to instructional practice.** Principals monitor classroom practice, and foster and encourage a culture of sharing good practice and the development of professional learning communities at school, with him or herself being a crucial point of reference in terms of instructional and pedagogical mastery.
- **Management of people and processes.** Principals focus on the effective management and use of materials and resources, including human resources, such as the recruitment, professional development and retention of teachers.

Where schools, through their principals, demonstrate effective and sustained leadership over these dimensions, it is believed they will be better positioned to improve achievement outcomes for students. As Townsend and MacBeath (2011) argue, leadership for learning is concerned with student outcomes, teacher development and professional motivation within a creative learning organization that nurtures a spirit of learning in an accessible and a safe environment; socializes learning through internal and external dialogue with researchers and practitioners; distributes and shares leadership and encourages personal leadership among staff and students; and fosters reflection and self-evaluation (MacBeath, 2008).

Securing effective instruction

As is commonly known, principals are directly accountable to students for the quality of education provided and for their achievement outcomes. As a result, in line with raising school attainment and improving achievement outcomes for individual students, principals will usually try to have in place the best possible staff team from the stock of persons available in terms of skills, experience, qualifications and 'personality fit'. Effective principals know that securing excellent outcomes for students and outstanding results for schools is also a function of the capacity of staff. One principal reflected on her school's decision to recruit teachers from overseas:

> We are located in an inner-city area of London with lots of migrant families. We've opted to recruit a lot of teachers from abroad because we believe they are better placed, in terms of language and culture, to help migrant students and families. They better understand the backgrounds and life experiences from which these pupils have come and we find these staff central to our work and to the success of a number of our pupils, specifically.
>
> Principal 2, England, female

As instructional leadership is concerned with students' achievement outcomes, most – if not all – principals, will make the professional development of their staff a key area of school policy and practice. In other words, the skills development and learning needs of staff should be taken seriously and appropriately linked to a school's development plan. It should be noted however that not all schools will be in a position to provide all staff with an opportunity to attend externally arranged and delivered continuing professional development (CPD) activities, although some are able to and therefore do. As a result, some schools may only be able to arrange and deliver CPD activities to staff internally. The merits of both approaches are not in debate and have been well articulated (Tomlinson, 1997). Nevertheless, some schools have found it more beneficial to combine internal and external approaches to CPD with the aim of 'keeping costs down' while arguably 'providing staff the best of both worlds'. Whatever the method, the relationship between staff development and achievement outcomes for students is a highly regarded one:

> We are big on outcomes for all pupils. And to give each child a good chance at achieving five good GCSEs and their best possible educational life chance, we invest heavily in staff development. The research is clear: there is a clear relationship between pupil outcomes and staff development and we take this seriously.
>
> Principal 5, England, male

Decisions about how staff professional development is organized and delivered can be a source of tension (Hirsh, 2010) and is a matter for each school. However, the importance of staff being sufficiently competent and confident to guide students to successful achievement outcomes is a matter not only for teachers and principals, but for an entire school community and for society as a whole. Despite the important issue of a school's approach to CPD and/or its (in)ability to fund a particular approach to CPD, what is significant here are the content and intended outcomes of a CPD activity. As Bubb and Earley (2007) propose, 'Effective continuing professional development is likely to consist of that which first and foremost enhances pupil outcomes, but which also helps to bring about changes in practice and improves teaching' (p. 4).

Spotlight 2: Remote Primary Two Jamaica – instructional leadership

Remote Primary Two is led by Mary* who is in her late thirties. This is her first appointment as a principal and she has been in post for five years. She has a bachelor's degree in education and a diploma in education. Remote Primary Two has four teachers, including Mary. Two teachers have master's qualifications. There are fewer than 50 students on roll. The school has two ancillary staff including a 'cook' and a 'cleaner'. The school does not have a 'watchman' or security guard and Mary does not have a secretary or an administrative assistant.

The school has an outside toilet for staff and two outside toilets for students (one each for girls and boys). It is located in a remote part of Jamaica with very limited vehicular access due to poor road conditions. The school sits on a beautiful parcel of land on a rise that overlooks the road. The land itself has several different fruit trees from which students and staff eat during crop. There is no piped water and there are no rivers nearby so students either fetch water from a nearby stand-pipe or parents purchase water from the water board. The school gets water delivered for free from the water board although deliveries are sporadic and unreliable. Nearly all parents of students at Remote Primary Two do not work and the literacy rate among parents is believed to be quite low. The majority of parents are local farmers.

Mary describes her school as having several challenges but also several opportunities. For example, in recent years several 'good' teachers have left due to the wear and tear the poor road conditions place on their vehicles and due to the lack of progression prospects. In addition, several parents have withdrawn their children from the school citing 'fear' for children due to the heavily forested area which surrounds the school and poor mobile telephone connectivity, which sometimes makes it difficult for them to be in contact with their children.

Despite a fall in school roll and despite a loss of some 'good teachers' Mary describes her school as achieving year-on-year improvements in both the Grade Four Literacy Test and the Grade Six Achievement Test (GSAT). Both tests are nationally administered. In addition to annual improvements in national tests, Mary describes her school as very 'quiet', 'a prime space for learning with very little distraction' and an 'excellent environment to focus on one-to-one or small group teaching and learning'.

Mary describes her staff as committed and enthusiastic. She also describes her parents as 'very supportive of what we do'. Mary's school has no electricity and no computers.

Resourcing effective instruction

Principals 'juggle' several tasks and roles and it is perhaps understandable that they should do this. However, they also juggle decision-making in respect of the allocation of scarce financial and other resources. For example, they juggle decisions about how to use and/or increase space for teaching and learning and/ or whether to increase space for recreation. Many of the decisions a principal will make will have implications for the quality and type of education experience provided to students, and thus secure the best achievement outcomes for them. Whereas it may be possible for a principal to make a straight material purchase at one time or another, they are not always able to do so and others who may be able to purchase material and resources may not always be able to get the best quality and/or adequate quantities.

Decisions about how to or how much to spend may not only be financial in nature but strategic, driven primarily by the needs of the school at a particular point in time and also by a school's ability to, in the future, fund other planned or unplanned projects. For example, should a school provide each student on a course with a textbook or should students be made to share? Should a school buy textbooks and rent these to students or should students bring their own? Is it more expedient to invest in additional classroom space or is it more expedient to purchase a school bus? If there is a library at the school, does it contain books that cover the range of subjects taught? Are the books in the school's library appropriate for students in terms of their age, gender, abilities and/or learning needs, and are they the latest and most up-to-date editions? Should a school stock a computer laboratory with new computers or should it use available funds to begin construction of an additional laboratory? These are but a few of the range of questions that require principals to consider a number of opportunity costs as they work to secure the best educational experience and outcomes for students. One principal reflects:

> My school is located in an inner-city area and sometimes school gets disrupted due to community uprisings. Sometimes school can be suspended for up to one week at a time. We wanted to improve our library stock to better serve our children, but as a staff, we took the decision to instead set up a virtual learning environment (VLE) platform so that when children are absent from school they can access the VLE. I know many students may not have computers at home but if some are able to access the VLE then I think we have made the right decision. Further, many parents have smartphones and other gadgets which they may be able to use to access the VLE platform.
>
> Principal 3, Jamaica, female

Principals and other leaders in education around the world are faced with similar curricula and other decisions that involve an element of opportunity cost. Decisions taken, however, are context dependent and are usually mediated in terms of economic, social, technological and other factors. Nevertheless, at the centre of curricula decisions is the requirement for principals to 'juggle' in the 'best interest' of students – a fundamental principle enshrined in the United Nations Convention on the Rights of the Child (UNCRC) (United Nations, 1989). Busher (2006) found resource allocation in schools was a principled, but value-laden activity (Simkins, 1997) and that resources were allocated to try to meet students' needs equitably, consistent with budgetary frameworks.

Spotlight 3: Creativity and resilience among teachers and students

A school is only as good as the people who work and study there. But there are different factors, both internal and external, that can negatively impact or even undermine a school's ability to deliver the kind of education it would want to provide to students or the kind which it thinks students should be getting. Social, economic, technological, political and economic factors are among the more obvious elements that can either negatively undermine or derail a school's plans to deliver a certain kind of educational quality and experience to learners.

> We have very creative teachers who know how to 'turn their hands'. Many students turn up without material and resources. In fact, sometimes the school itself is unable to provide or purchase the required material and resources. But, we have to find a way. We have to find a way to provide students with the education they need so they can stand a better chance in life later. We can't roll over and simply complain. We have to ensure students get what they come here for. We have to let the community know that, despite not having 'this' and 'that', we are still open for business.
>
> Principal 8, Jamaica, female

Despite the limitations placed on schools by the various factors, be they implicit or explicit, principals have highlighted two important things in terms of how teachers approach and fulfil their job roles. First, the creativity and commitment of teachers in the face of a lack of resources. Second, the attitude of teachers towards 'satisficing' or 'making do', rather than being preoccupied with or distracted by what a school does *not* have. This is a powerful counter-narrative that shifts the discourse and the focus of teachers away from the 'half empty glass' by placing a higher premium on what a school *can* achieve with what's available rather than on what it can't achieve based on what's not available.

Monitoring and supporting classroom practice

Schools exist for the development of the human talent. That is, schools exist to play a leading role in the shaping of the educational, social and moral aspects of learners. Principals are well aware of these most important roles of education and schools, and as a result many make the monitoring of teaching and learning a key internal accountability activity delivered through formal and informal means. Through formal activities such as lesson or classroom observations, or informal activities such as 'learning walks', principals and other staff with responsibility for behaviour and/or learning in a particular area or discipline can assess 'what is happening in the classroom'. Whereas lesson observations, whether formal or informal, can lead to the discovery of good practice, they are also useful for helping to identify, target and support improvements to poor practice wherever this is found (Assessment Reform Group, 1999). In the words of one principal:

> The pupils are the most important constituent in my school, and they are the reason we are here. My staff are fully aware that lessons must be well planned and assessment opportunities given regularly so as to measure progress. We are accountable for the future of those children.
>
> Principal 1, England, male

Poor practice among teachers can lead to devastating consequences for learners. Uncovering poor practice, whether through formal or informal lesson observations, or from or in conjunction with student feedback, is an important issue principals usually seek to address without delay. This is because principals want students to get the best provision possible and for students to be 'on track' to achieving their full potential. Teachers failing to complete the curriculum; teachers not covering the curriculum in a timely manner allowing for revision; teachers not undertaking marking and assessment; teachers not making use of technology where available; teachers not using up-to-date teaching methods and material in their lessons; and teachers not providing detailed feedback to students have all been cited by principals in this work as examples of poor practice uncovered through monitoring exercises.

Feedback = feedforward

As mentioned earlier, schools have a duty to develop and nurture human talent. To do this effectively, principals and those in charge of teaching and learning, whether throughout school or in an area or subject discipline, must feed back to teachers about their performance, and teachers in turn, feed back to students about their performance, in an attempt to improve the overall effectiveness and standards of a school. Miller (2013c) describes this process as 'feedback equals feedforward' (p. 1). Crucially, this process supports personal development through constructive critique and dialogue. Starratt (1999) argues that learning is an active process rather than a consumerist one and that it is students, not teachers, who have 'the work of sense making, of producing knowledge suggested by the curriculum, of performing that knowledge in a variety of assessable products, of explaining how those performances and production reveal their understanding' (p. 23). Successful principals understand and apply this principle. They also understand the needs of their teachers – they listen to them; they anticipate their questions and respond to them in a way that is supportive, aimed at building their individual and collective capacities. Similarly, successful principals have a responsibility to provide teachers with appropriate skills for providing feedback to students on their work. As Hattie (2002, p. 8) notes:

> Feedback ... is essential. When students face learning challenges, there is a higher probability that they will need and seek feedback to which teachers can provide direction. Classroom relationships need to support students to seek this feedback. Teachers, critically, also need to become 'learners of their own teaching', using feedback from students on what they know, what they understand and when they have misconceptions, in order to refine their teaching. School leaders in turn need to be 'as great a teacher [as] your teachers, as great a learner as your teachers, and the person who provides the goalposts for excellence'.

The practice of providing feedback is smart and pragmatic and the role of the principal in modelling and/or otherwise supporting the skills acquisition and/or development of teachers (e.g. in providing feedback to students) is vital to all teachers, but especially those at the beginning and/or early phase of their teaching career, who may be in search of a source of direction and sense of motivation.

Principal as teacher

Whereas the particular characteristics of a school may make it difficult or impossible for a principal to continue to have a teaching role, there are those who, despite their busy offices and schedule, ensure they teach at least one lesson weekly so as to be up-to-date with the cut and thrust of classroom practice. Not only do they feel that being in the classroom helps to 'keep their ears to the ground', they also feel they can better express solidarity with teachers. Principals perceived themselves first and foremost as part of a community of teachers, not separated from it by their post as principal. Furthermore, they wanted to sustain and enhance their colleagues' and students' performances through being 'actively involved' in classroom practice.

> I run a school with just under 2,000 students so I no longer get a chance to teach. I would like to, but with all the meetings I have, and with all the problem-solving and strategizing that I need to do, I simply have to defer classroom teaching no matter how small. There will be too many urgent meetings that would interrupt my teaching or cause me to miss lessons.
>
> Principal 1, England, male

An observation made as far back as 1991 by Jones and Hayes of principals in the UK is that in smaller schools principals tended to be involved in teaching, and this was also found to be the case with principals in this study.

> My school has just under 50 students and I am a part of a staff team of five. I choose to teach because it is important for me to model practice and for my teachers to see and feel that we are in it together; so I can see what's happening in the classroom for myself: how students are learning; how they are behaving and what strategies are needed to be put in place to support teaching and learning.
>
> Principal 4, Jamaica, female

According to Gardner and Laskin (1995, p. 41):

> The ultimate impact of the leader depends on the particular story she/he relates or embodies and the receptions to that story on the part of the audience ... Since audiences come equipped with many stories that have already been told and retold ... the stories of the leader ... must compete with many extant stories; and if the new stories are to succeed, they must transplant, suppress, complement, or in some measure outweigh the earlier stories, as well as contemporary counterstories.

Although principals reported that increased administrative workload prevented them doing (more) teaching, and although '... managerial and administrative duties were beginning to take their toll on the curriculum leadership of principals' (Great Britain, 1991, para. 48, p. 8), there was obvious tension among them, not least due to the demands and realities of the job roles as performed in their individual contexts, but also due to what each principal believed was a priority. Nevertheless, as Hall and Southworth (1997) remind us, 'Whilst there is more to manage and administer, the long standing expectation at the level of national policy that heads should be curriculum leaders continues unaltered' (p. 156).

Spotlight 4: Principals as active teachers

Principals in both case study countries and possibly the world over are finding it increasingly difficult to get involved directly in teaching due to other job demands. Nevertheless, not all principals feel it is permissible or even acceptable, despite the increased workload, for them not to teach even a small proportion of lessons each week. They suggest that when principals and other school leaders are (able to be) directly involved in teaching, it provides a number of important benefits to the school as a whole:

1. It provides first-hand knowledge of what is going on in classrooms and possibly throughout the school.
2. It demonstrates to colleagues that principals and other school leaders know what challenges they are faced with.
3. It allows principals and other school leaders to see, first-hand, the types of learners at the school and whether their needs are being appropriately provided for.
4. It provides direct accounts of and engagement with behavioural issues faced by staff.

I teach one class each week, but that's about all I can do. I would love to do more but with just over 500 students and over 80 staff, there are a lot of other things to keep me occupied. I am a teacher's teacher and therefore, no matter how pressing my schedule gets, I would still want to teach. This keeps me actively involved in the teaching and learning process where I can have a first-hand handle on things my teachers may find challenging. Besides, I think if students are taught by senior staff, they are more likely to behave better and come to class prepared for learning.

Principal 6, England, male

The view of this principal is rather insightful. It is true that principals and other school leaders are finding it increasingly difficult to be directly involved in teaching and learning. It is also true that this difficulty potentially robs them of direct opportunities to informally monitor teaching, learning and behaviour, and to show solidarity with their colleagues. Nevertheless, this view of 'leadership from the front' is an important one, demonstrated in terms of 'being in the thick of things' from which principals can draw insights in order to better support the needs of teachers and students, and in order to be able to say to staff '...in addition to the legal authority, I also have moral authority to challenge your practice'.

The fact principals want to be more involved in teaching and learning activities is important for both the policy and practice environments of schooling. In terms of the policy environment, it suggests a re-think in relation to the wave of new managerialism bedevilling principals, and from a practice perspective, it underline's Coulson's (1986) observation that 'the readiness of head(teachers) to put time in(to) classrooms is valued by most teachers. It makes a recognisable area of his (her) work more visible and shows a willingness to attempt what he (she) advocates: to "come down on the shop floor", "get his hands dirty", and "practice what he preaches"' (pp. 64–5).

Leading from the front and by example is an effective hallmark of instructional and other forms of leadership practice. Evidence from principals in this book suggests they practise this kind of leadership, although work roles do not allow some to be as involved as they would have liked. They understand the importance of possessing 'moral authority' and 'integrity' and in being seen as 'credible' by teachers and others in a school community. They also want to be seen as leaders in curriculum innovation at school and as points of reference for staff (McHugh & McMullan, 1995). Despite a longing to become more involved in teaching – even a single lesson each week – some principals were sceptical that this would happen since current reforms in education have led to their role being constructed as 'anti-teaching' and 'pro-managerial'; a situation manifest in the school leadership landscape in England, resulting in some schools moving from having a head*teacher* or lead educationalist to having a chief executive.

Achieving in difficulty

Despite managerialist notions and increased accountability measures, educational reforms in both developed and developing countries have shown some degree of sensitivity towards improving schools in difficult or challenging circumstances. Many schools, particularly in socially neglected communities, are confronted by a range of socioeconomic issues including high levels of unemployment among adults, physical and mental health issues, skills migration and low educational achievement. Schools in these areas also face problems of poor student behaviour, higher than normal staff turnover and a poor physical environment (Chapman & Harris, 2004). As pointed out by Gray (2001): '[W]e don't really know how much more difficult it is for schools serving disadvantaged communities to improve because much of the improvement research has ignored this dimension – that it is more difficult, however, seems unquestionable' (p. 33).

Schools facing multiple challenges may be less open to critical scrutiny or exposure since they are, most often, the schools where performance and achievement among students is below the expected standard. As a result, principals in these schools have to work harder, rallying an entire school community to join forces to improve and to remain effective (Reynolds et al., 2006).

> The National Education Inspectorate recently inspected my school. We received a grade of 'Unsatisfactory'. We have done our reflections and we are working as a team of staff and with partners from outside to turn things round in the shortest possible time.
>
> Principal 10, Jamaica, female

> Turning around a school that is deemed to be 'failing' is no easy feat. Staffing decisions, subject fit, staff experience, qualifications and numbers are critical. But so is the adequacy of resources, support from the governors, support from the local authority, parents' support, pupil attitudes and a stable, supportive, multi-layered approach to school leadership.
>
> Principal 2, England, female

It is not impossible to 'buck the trend' of poor performance and achievement for schools in difficult circumstances. Some schools have faced difficult circumstances and are able to add significant value to levels of student achievement and learning, where commitment to do so is beyond 'normal efforts' (Maden & Hillman, 1996). One principal observes:

> I have led the turnaround of two schools that were placed in 'Special Measures' by Ofsted. Each school has meant different challenges but each school also provide exciting opportunities for me to change things, to raise expectations and attainment and to build capacity throughout the school.
>
> Principal 6, England, male

A common thread among principals was how challenging it is to turn around a school deemed to be operating in difficult circumstances. But it is not impossible. They point to a range of socioeconomic, student demographic, parental involvement and resource related factors that are often ignored when 'passing judgement' on schools. Similarly, they cite a range of processes which may need changing, although they suggest 'leadership', 'teaching' and 'monitoring of teaching' will be singled out. Nevertheless, when a school is deemed to be in 'difficult circumstances', it cannot be business as usual for anyone associated with that school, especially the principal who will have to develop and lead an agenda for improvement (Whitty & Anders, 2012).

Spotlight 5: Leading learning in a 'failed' or 'failing' school

A fundamental purpose of schooling is the provision of education and to the development of skills in learners. Providing the kind of education that meets these aims however can be problematic – from being unable to find appropriately qualified staff (in sufficient numbers), to the physical plant of a school being run down, to lack of resources. These are but few of the factors that can derail a school's ambition of providing learners with education and skills. But there are others too, such as being labelled as 'failing' or 'unsatisfactory', or being described as 'in special measures' or 'requiring improvement'.

> It is very hard leading a school labelled as being in 'special measures'. The label alone can cause staff, students and parents to shun the school. Convincing parents that you are still capable of securing quality outcomes for their children will be more of an uphill struggle. And motivating staff and students who remain can be extremely difficult. And facing your colleagues, fellow principals, who do not have to 'wear this label', can lead to serious depression as you feel so incompetent, so out of place.
>
> Principal 2, England, female

As more and more education systems introduce education inspectorates and increase public accountability through inspections, the 'naming and shaming' of schools believed to be performing below national or expected standards might be expected to continue. The merits of naming and shaming, and the debates surrounding such a practice, cannot be resolved in this book. However, principals are clear that in addition to them finding this practice 'debilitating', it also runs counter to solving the problem of achieving quality education, potentially leading to other problems for a school that has been 'named and shamed' and for other schools and units elsewhere in the education system. Instead of labelling schools, principals instead proposed a typology of 'close up' monitoring and support that was transparent, time bound, included multiple stakeholders and took account of contextual factors.

Achieving when location is a problem

Geographical isolation of rural schools, gang feuds and uprisings in inner-city communities, selective local educational systems, lack of or ineffective support from an education ministry or department and low levels of formal qualifications for teachers can all challenge and hamper the prospects of longer-term sustained improvement for some schools (Ofsted, 2009). This is not to suggest that schools in challenging circumstances and areas cannot improve, or do not do well in the first place; rather, it is worth noting that the context of schooling in these circumstances is significantly different compared with those schools located in urban and suburban areas and operating in/under more favourable conditions, socially and economically.

> Our intake is relatively mixed in terms of ethnicities. However, we have far more pupils from socially neglected communities and many more pupils receiving free school meals now than in the two years previous. Our school is relatively well resourced but often pupils turn up unkempt, unprepared and without homework. This creates a range of challenges for us as a school, but we know that what is happening to the children is connected to what's happening at home. Despite the challenges, however, some parents are very supportive and some pupils have achieved really well and have gone on to university.
>
> Principal 2, England, female

Leading a school in a location of challenge can be an exciting thing. Conversely, it can be quite demanding. Principals and those who work in such schools are expected to transform the fortunes of a school in the shortest possible time, ensuring students receive the best possible education. In the UK, recent research by the Department for Environment and Rural Affairs (DEFRA, 2012) acknowledges that schools in rural areas face a number of challenges faced by similar schools located in urban areas.

> My school has just over 40 students and we are based in a deep rural community. We have good water supply that is trucked in and good electricity connection despite our location. We are somewhat challenged though as many good teachers will not come so far into the rural areas to work and we lack many of the resources and facilities that schools in urban and suburban areas have.
>
> Principal 4, Jamaica, female

From the rural/remote extreme to leading in an urban inner-city area, one principal highlights:

> My school is often affected due to gang-related violence. I can't do anything about that – that's the job for the police and politicians. But I make it my business to get to know the leaders of major gangs and say to them, 'You can't hold my staff and students to ransom. School must go on ….' As a result, if there is an uprising, staff and students usually have a 'free passage' to go to and from school, unless things get really bad and we have to suspend classes.
>
> Principal 10, Jamaica, female

Like any organization, whether privately or publicly run, location is a key factor in a school's success or failure. The immediate environs help to shape its reputation, and establish its sense of purpose and identity. Leading, working in or attending a school described as being in 'challenging circumstances' can result in demotivation and loss of focus. The school board, and the principal, especially, are responsible for devising a workable plan that can be deployed in the shortest possible time that will retain, if not raise, the confidence of teachers, students and parents. For any plan to work, there has to be support from staff, students, parents where necessary, and external agencies, underlining Grace's (2001) view that schools alone are not responsible for their success, but rather for schools to succeed against the odds there needs to be 'interlocking of support agencies, i.e. a form of social and pedagogical capital that is differentially available to schools in different school situations' (p. 234).

Spotlight 6: Achieving in an isolated location

There are many good reasons why some schools located in rural and remote communities do not do as well as others located in suburban and urban areas and vice versa. It is not uncommon to find a language of deficit being used to describe schools located in rural and remote areas and some schools in 'inner-city' areas or urban centres, both from those who attend and work in them and also from others who have first-hand experience of them. Whereas this narrative may, in and of itself, be true, it does not by any means represent the full picture of what goes on in all schools located in rural, remote or inner-city communities. While the location of a school can be a serious hindrance to learning and teaching, this is not always the case.

> Our location is a prime environment for learning. We are located in a relatively rural community so our students and teachers will have very little distraction on a daily basis. Although we lack many of the basic facilities and amenities, we do provide learners with a rich and varied educational experience to the best of our ability. Many parents do not work, and the majority are farmers, but our Parent Teachers' Association is very active and we get parents involved in all we do. So, at this school, there is a genuine year-on-year improvement in students' performance in school and national examinations. Having said that, we have also had cases over the past two to three years where staff and students have left the school citing the school's rural and somewhat inaccessible location.
>
> Principal 8, Jamaica, female

The location paradox has been highlighted by this principal – an experience probably shared by many principals in other parts of the world. A school's location can result in long queues of parents wanting their child to join; but a school's location can also result in many parents not wanting to send their children to certain schools in the first place. Furthermore, a school's location coupled with other social and environmental factors, such as access to electricity, roadways, hospitals and telecommunications infrastructure, can lead to retention issues among both staff and students.

Reflection

School systems all over the world have two features that at some stage will play a dominant role in the life of most students that pass through them. That is, the preparation for and the presentation for public examinations. The attainment of students in these examinations provides a prominent measure of both student and school success, often used to rank schools and to allocate resources. Whether or not one approves of examination outcomes as the basis of the assessment of the effectiveness of schools, they are subsequently used in the selection and channeling of students in post-secondary educational and occupational careers, which means that they have real effects on the lives of students once they have left school (Reynolds & Cuttance, 1992), which in turn means schools and students have to be well prepared for them to begin with.

The case studies presented in this chapter show stark contrasts between and within schools, based on variation in size, type and location, contrasts which may not be readily acknowledged in performance league tables. But these variations and differences need to be recognized and considered and their implications for the practice of school leadership examined in the context in which individual schools operate. Otherwise, 'writing about school leadership may remain too general and become unconvincing to practitioners because it does not recognise nor reflect the contextual nature of their work' (Hall & Southworth, 1997, p. 158). Nevertheless, for a school to be successful in securing quality achievement outcomes for all students, principals must be centrally and integrally involved in all aspects of schooling, influencing the teaching strategies used by teachers and monitoring the academic progress and behaviour of students. In the words of Alexander et al. (1992), principals 'should take a lead in ensuring high quality provision, monitoring teaching and learning and providing a vision of what their schools should become' (p. 47) – a view that not only underlines the principal's role as an instructional leader but fundamentally that as a school leader.

3

Diversity Leadership

[I]ncreasingly the discourse of special education is being drawn upon to frame discussions and policy concerning educational failure. This illustrates a dilemma, not restricted to developing countries, but acutely experienced in these settings. On the other hand, the need for improved and targeted learning support coupled with the training of teachers, particularly in the mainstream sector, to work effectively with children with a range of special educational needs is very evident. On the other hand, the language of special education can itself impede an analysis of more deep-seated problems in respect of both funding and policy for improving the quality of education for all children.

Armstrong et al., 2010, p. 9

We should be talking more about how advancing race and ethnicity issues are not only taught generally in England, and globally, through both cross-curricular practice and through the subject of citizenship ... Education must continue to have a key role in the positive promotion of immigrants within all cultures and societies through cross-curricula and citizenship studies. Teachers and lecturers need to have the training and Continuing Professional Development to teach diversity so that issues concerning social equity and social justice can be addressed with confidence rather than with fear.

Race & Lander, 2014, p. 225

Introduction

Principals are the chief custodians of a school's social fibre. That is they, by what they say and do, and in how they treat others, send a message to others inside and outside a school community about their stance on issues such as respect, fairness, equality and justice. Principals play a key role in building and defining the ethos of a school. In other words, what a school stands for and what it wishes to be known for are central to how a principal constructs the internal environment of a school, appropriately making references to international and national policies that he/she interprets and applies at school level. A principal has a fundamental duty of care to all members of a school community, whether they be teachers, students or other adults working at a school. This duty of care is the same for each person and is often delivered through words and actions, backed by appropriate school-level policies.

A principal simultaneously creates and tells a story of himself/herself and the school they lead by the conditions of work and study staff and students endure or enjoy; through the meaningfulness of their engagement with staff and/or students; in the way they treat staff and/or students; and based on the nature and quality of the educational opportunities available to members of a school community. Schools are microcosms of society and as a result they are influenced by the collective beliefs, practices and other patterns of socialization within society. Put differently, a school may be thought of as a melting pot; a community crossroads where views and practices are transmitted, shaped, contested, re-shaped and re-transmitted. But a school can also be seen as much more than that. As McAllister and Hadjri (2013) put it, 'To a child, a school is many things: not just a place for learning, but also a place of new experiences, a test bed to develop social skills and a supportive environment in which to develop and find themselves' (p. 63).

A school however is not a place where all views must contend equally, nor is it a place where all views must contend. A school, as an agent for socialization and change has an important role in teaching and promoting inclusion, gender, racial and ethnic equality, social harmony and cohesion, tolerance and respect and justice for all, established on the principles of meritocracy and of equal rights. These values derive from and are echoed in the six overlapping themes of dignity and justice, development, environment, culture, gender and participation, as reflected in the United Nations Universal Declaration of Human Rights (UDHR) (1948).

- **Dignity and justice:** these are foundational promises for each and every human being set out in the UDHR. The notion of dignity lies at the heart of human rights and underlines the values of respect, tolerance and understanding. The notion of justice and the equality of everyone before the law appears throughout the UDHR, underlining its core values of non-discrimination and equality which represent a commitment to universal justice and the inherent human dignity of all.

- **Development:** poverty is a key issue that has potential to undermine the realization of the full potential of individuals and societies. The UDHR shares a vision of the world in which everyone, no matter where they live and who they are, has equal opportunity to grow and develop in freedom and equality and to their full potential. The UDHR also makes clear the responsibility of nations and peoples to assist each other, through individual and joint actions in order to create a social and international order that enables the enjoyment of all human rights – civil, cultural, economic, political and social.

- **Environment:** the UDHR does not specifically mention the environment. However, over the past six decades there has been more consistent recognition of environmental degradation and how changes in the environment can have a significant impact on ability of humans to enjoy their human rights. It is clear that the actions of nations, communities, businesses and individuals can dramatically affect the rights of others, because damaging the environment can curtail the rights of people, near and far, to securing and/or enjoying a healthy life.

- **Culture:** human rights underlines the belief that culture is an invaluable commodity that is linked to human identity. Humans can learn from each other and in return benefit from each other's culture. Article 27 of the UDHR states, 'everyone has the right freely to participate in the cultural life of the community'. By implication, no one therefore has the right to dominate, direct or eradicate that culture or impose theirs upon anyone else.

- **Gender:** the UDHR acknowledges that men and women are not the same but insists on their right to be equal before the law and treated without discrimination. Gender equality is not a 'women's issue' but refers to the equal rights, responsibilities and opportunities of women and men, girls and boys, and should concern and fully engage men as well as women. The right to be free of discrimination on the grounds of sex is specifically set out in Article 2.

- **Participation:** individuals, no matter whether they live in the developed or developing world, each have an equal right to take a full part in the life of their community. Without participation, individuals cannot enjoy and experience the wide range of rights and freedoms that the UDHR attempts to deliver. Article 21 assures this right, recognizing that the voices of people who are often excluded should be heard and heeded, especially those marginalized or discriminated against due to disability, race, religion, gender, descent, age or on other grounds.

The UDHR is supplemented by several other legal agreements at international and national levels, with many countries also adopting international laws into their domestic provisions – for example, the UNCRC (1989). This chapter will consider these issues in greater detail in the sections that follow.

Positioning inclusion

In countries all around the world, the inclusion of individuals with special education needs and disabled individuals have become a major focus for governments. Whether this new focus is a product or outcome of recent or indeed current reforms in the global educational environment is debatable. Nevertheless, until relatively recently, the separation between mainstream and special education was premised on the idea of different kinds of education for different kinds of students (Armstrong et al., 2010). Whereas the traditional view of 'special education' and how this was delivered was challenged mainly by disabled individuals themselves, and interest groups acting on their behalf, it appeared that policy-makers became interested in social inclusion issues because of a belief that education can play a significant role in promoting social harmony and respect in increasingly diverse societies (Ainscow et al., 2006). These views are not only to be found in developed countries, but also in developing countries where disabled individuals and their supporters consistently argue that 'special education' limits opportunities for disabled individuals as citizens due to the fact that the label 'special' implies they have intellectual, social and/or physical deficits.

In developed countries such as in the UK, the idea of 'inclusive education' is one that has challenged the role of special education, driven mainly by interest groups, which advocates a model of 'inclusive education' built on social justice, respect for and the protection of human rights. In developing countries, inclusive education has been used rather differently, sometimes to mean social justice linked to UNESCO's policy on 'Education for All'. According to Armstrong et al. (2010), this approach has advocacy at its heart, although when translated into national settings within the developing world, there might be a noticeable gap between policy options and resource availability and allocations.

Nevertheless, as pointed out earlier, a principal, through his or her leadership, has a critical role in promoting inclusive practices at school. The United Nations Convention on the Rights of Persons with Disabilities (UNCRPD) (2006) proposes that: 'State Parties recognise the right of persons with disabilities to education. With a view to realising this right without discrimination and on the basis of equal opportunity, State Parties shall ensure an inclusive education system at all levels and lifelong learning' (Article 24).

Inclusion in its simplest and purest form encapsulates all persons whether adults or children, recognizing and affirming their limitless potential. In the UK, Ofsted found that in schools where the central ethos was centered on inclusion, students achieved more and better results, and where this occurred, leadership was shown to be a significant factor (Ofsted, 2004).

> Within the last two years, we had students at school with various physical disabilities. We have students with visual and hearing impairment and we have students who cannot walk properly due to cerebral palsy. The SEN department mobilized a lot of support from staff for these students and I would say we were successful. However, I felt we were being reactive and superficial and not thinking long term. Working closely with the SEN/EAL team and with the local authority, we developed a school-wide inclusion policy that was implemented last year – with lots of support from the governors.
>
> Principal 6, England, male

Brown and Conrad (2007) suggest that in Trinidad & Tobago, effective principals employ a number of strategies to subvert the (education) system in order to be effective. These subverting activities, they argue, have become necessary in order to overcome the restrictive capacities imposed by an overarching bureaucracy that has not changed in any meaningful way since the end of colonialization (Brown & Lavia, 2013). Principals have remained locked in a constricting bureaucracy that does not allow for 'practice exercised under the label of leadership or managerial autonomy' (Brown & Conrad, 2007, p. 194).

> We have a couple of students at school who are HIV+. We do not prevent them from taking lessons in food preparation and or physical education, for example. It's their entitlement. Their HIV+ status is not public knowledge and only myself, my deputy and the guidance counsellor knows. As a leadership team, we do our best to protect our HIV+ students as well as all other students from activities that could impair their schooling experience or cause harm or injury to themselves or anyone else.
>
> Principal 10, Jamaica, female

In order for disabled students to thrive and to be included in the mainstream, there has to be a pedagogical approach that recognizes each student as unique. However, to be successful, this pedagogical approach needs to be supported by adequate funding that can make resourcing (more) inclusive in mainstream schools. Principals shared concerns for students' physical safety due to varying long-term disabilities for which schools did not have (adequate) resources to (sufficiently) address. For example, more and more schools were enrolling students who use wheelchairs to get around, but as there were no lifts at school, students in wheelchairs relied heavily on a teaching assistant or another student to help them from 'point A to point B'. In other cases, although a school had functional typewriters, principals were unable to purchase photocopiers and/or computers so that materials for visually impaired students could be photocopied and/or printed in a 'large enough font size', and for other school processes to be improved.

Positioning race and ethnicity

The terms 'race' and 'ethnicity' are acknowledged as problematic but are also commonly used to identify the issues of colour and cultural racism with which this section of the chapter is concerned. Similarly, diversity is contested and refers to the existence of different cultures, ethnicities, socioeconomic levels, sexual orientations, abilities or races within a group or organization (Yukl, 2012). In fact, some individuals prefer to use the term 'inclusion' instead of diversity, in trying to highlight that organizations need to include as many diverse people as possible (DuBrin, 2010).

Due to the continuing march of globalization, school systems and principals in both developing and developed countries face some degree of exposure to issues of ethnic diversity. In the United Kingdom, and in other multi-ethnic, multi-racial countries, race and ethnicity issues continue to influence the experience of children and adults at all levels of the education system in a variety of respects. These include, for example, participation in education, academic achievement, employment and social mobility, social interactions and parental involvement.

Discrimination of any kind weakens the social fibre of any institution and of society as a whole. The Convention against Discrimination in Education (UNESCO, 1960) promotes equal treatment for anyone involved in education at any level in every society. As mentioned earlier, schools are microcosms of society where the values and practices of the society in which they exist are transmitted, contested, debated, shaped, re-shaped and re-transmitted. Furthermore, schools have a transformative role – to agitate, to challenge, to question, to dismantle and to change old and contrary tendencies and behaviours, replacing them with more socially acceptable and inclusive ways of being. Put differently, ways of being that respect, extend and simultaneously fulfil the social order for individuals and society.

Racial discrimination

Principals reported different levels and degrees of interaction with race and ethnicity related issues ranging from students' interactions at school to staff recruitment and progression. They reported being 'against all forms of discrimination' with some describing racial/ethnic discrimination as evil.

> We've had a few incidents of racism at school targeted mainly towards teachers from overseas. These have been most unfortunate. Pupils sometimes are misguided at home and we at school can only do our best to reinforce that for us we value each member of the school community equally . . .
>
> Principal 9, England, female

> The senior leadership team at my school mirrors the student population. And so does the teaching and other categories of staff. It is important, as part of my overriding philosophy, and for the school's emotional health that ethnic, gender diversity and other diversities are represented at the highest level of decision making; and where appropriate this includes disabled individuals.
>
> Principal 5, England, male

To help tackle racial and ethnic problems and stereotypes, some principals choose to work in inner-city schools with large minority ethnic populations. Recognizing the bi-directional flows of culture and the importance of social cohesion, one principal in East London suggested her preference is to work only in inner-city schools:

> I prefer to work only in inner-city schools. That's my personal pledge. Schools in inner cities are culturally rich. I am always moved by the richness of cultures and the opportunity to promote sociocultural learning. I am learning so much and I would not want to work in schools located outside an inner-city community. I feel I can both learn more and contribute more here.
>
> Principal 2, England, female

A principal from an urban area in North London provides an ethnic, racial and culturally embracing stance:

> Our school is made up of 42 languages and over 25 nationalities in terms of staff and students. Staff and students at school, are the school. We value each one individually. We do not favour anyone more or less highly because of social class, gender or ethnicity, for example. We are one school; for each pupil and for all pupils.
>
> Principal 6, England, male

The majority of views in this section on racial discrimination relate to English principals, perhaps due to England's multi-ethnic/racial make-up compared with Jamaica. Some principals were somewhat 'embarrassed' to talk about race/ethnic discrimination issues. Whereas they accepted that racial discrimination was still fairly extant in the United Kingdom, they preferred to talk about 'how far we've come' as a country. Some also pointed to the Equality Act (2010) as an important tool in helping to fight racism and discrimination at the school level, while arguing that racism claims were often *perceived* rather than real. Such tensions warrant further investigation beyond this book. Nevertheless, Hill, writing as far back as 2001 about schooling and equality in England, argues that 'Whether equality becomes a fact of life depends on how valued it is, on whether it is seen as an improving or destructive force within social, cultural and economic relationships' (Hill, 2001, p. 7). Furthermore, Bhavani et al. (2005) conclude there is (still) an urgent need to tackle many types of racism in the UK, in particular 'situated racism', which refers to prejudice and unequal treatment and 'elite racism', which exists in the form of stereotyped assumptions and generalizations about different ethnic groups, which are reproduced by public figures and by the media and which have a major influence on public attitudes and behaviours, including those in schools.

Discriminatory practices and progression

Discriminatory practices in the area of teacher promotion and progression have featured in debates about school leadership in recent decades, both in developed (Earley et al., 2002, 2012; Shah & Shaikh, 2010) and in developing countries (Miller, 2014). Based on studies which examined the progression of black and minority ethnic (BME) teachers, Earley et al. (2002, 2012), found that teachers of BME origin experienced adverse selection in terms of being selected/appointed to positions of leadership in schools.

> We are a diverse school and we actively seek out ways to be inclusive to everyone. We support the career direction of all staff so long as their ambitions can move us closer towards achieving our educational goals for all students. For us, it matters not if you are black, white or Asian – what matter is your capacity to lead; to turn things around for students; to positively influence the outcomes of our school and students.
>
> Principal 1, England, male

Although stating this was not the case, principals admitted being accused of not employing and/or promoting teachers based on their religious affiliation:

We promote staff based on merit although for certain positions, like that of head of religious studies, you will need to be a member of the faith group that operates the school. And we are a faith school. However, we promote and affirm the value of hard work to our students, showing them that merit is what is going to get them the best job and not their physical appearance, ethnic origin or sexual appearance.

Principal 8, Jamaica, female

Both English and Jamaican principals suggested that religion was important in some instances to gaining a promotion to certain roles such as heading a department or leading a school. Shah and Shaikh (2010) reported that, for Muslims in the UK, their religion presented itself as a major hurdle when applying for a post as a principal in a non-Muslim school. Miller (2013b) reported that, in Jamaica, teachers who did not belong to a faith group that operates faith-led schools, such as Catholics, Anglicans, Baptists and Methodists, were less likely to get an appointment as a principal in these schools.

We promote staff strictly on the basis of merit. There is no other criteria. We are concerned about quality outcomes for all students in equal measure. We do not promote teachers based on years of service or based on any other perceived criteria. We promote entirely on the basis of merit.

Principal 10, Jamaica, female

Miller (2013b) also reported that some teachers in Jamaica believe selection/promotion to the rank of principal is in part due to social connections that could either work for or against aspirants. This point was reinforced by the education minister, Revd Ronald Thwaites, who, during a speech to parliament on 13 January 2015 noted that 'It is extremely important that while we respect seniority or other ascriptive requirements, what church you belong to, what politics you join can no longer play a part in determining educational leadership' (Gleaner, 2015). Miller replicated his 2013 Jamaican study among a group of principals and teachers in England who also confirmed that 'religious affiliation' and 'social connections' were dominant forces in the promotion/selection process since the 'networks' were at work (Miller, 2014). It should however be noted that Miller's findings (2013b, 2014) do not directly apply to the principals whose stories and experiences are the basis of this book. Instead, they relate more broadly to the experiences of teachers and principals in the Jamaican and English educational systems. One principal in this case study confirmed that religious affiliation does play a role in the selection process for certain job roles at her school – a faith-based school, for example, being in charge of the religious studies curriculum.

Spotlight 7: Inclusive employment practices

Staffing a school is not easy, for a school is a place rich in diversities. Although important, principals have to be careful their staffing decisions are not based entirely on a single characteristic (e.g. gender), unless this is absolutely necessary. In many respects, schools mirror society and much of what happens in them also mirrors what happens in society. As a result, principals are well aware that they have a responsibility, by their actions and decision-making in schools, to challenge practices in society that are potentially injurious to good order and social cohesion.

> Sometimes our staff question the decisions we take about staffing in terms of recruitment and promotion. Why did this person not get a promotion or a particular job? Why are there so few staff from this or that ethnic origin in promoted posts? Why are there so few staff from this or that ethnic origin on the leadership team? We are keen that our school should mirror society in terms of who attends, who works therein and who is entrusted to leadership or other positions of responsibility. However, our appointment and promotion decisions are based on purely on merit . . .
>
> Principal 9, England, female

Discrimination and/or the perception of discrimination of any kind in a school, whether directed by or towards students or staff, can weaken a principal's and also a school's ability to focus on teaching and learning and the provision of quality education. Principals in this case study were mindful of the potential for backlash that could arise from perceived or actual discriminatory decision-making while balancing the rights of students to an education 'fit for purpose'.

Positioning social class

Across the world, in both developing and developed countries, children have very different chances in life based on their social and economic circumstances. Throughout a child's development their life chances are influenced by both their previous experiences and by current factors such as their family circumstances. The Fabian Society (2006) outlines four influences affecting children across their life course: 'parental and family factors; neighbourhood effects and public services; features of the socio-economic inequalities; and wider public policy interventions' (p. 49). It is not difficult to see how wealthier parents will be able to bring their resources to bear to the benefit of their children. They can also afford to live in better quality accommodation and in safer, more prosperous areas, with better public services, transport and amenities.

Poorer families will usually live where they can afford to, which may mean lower standards of housing, safety, transport or education. But if the general nature of the relationship between such family characteristics and children's outcomes is widely known, it is much more difficult to understand how things work in detail. In other words, there is still much more to discover and understand about the relative effects of specific factors such as parents' incomes and education and about the specific way that certain problems may, on their own, or in combination, curtail opportunities (Blow et al., 2005). This section will not consider these issues in any depth, rather the interplay between and among these factors; how they influence students and therefore the delivery of education; and the response of school leaders to these issues, since a school is a site where poverty, deprivation and other forms of lack are often made manifest.

> We deliver a mainstream education in a comprehensive school. That is – we have students from rich and poor backgrounds mixing; we also have students from different nationalities and ethnic origins and we have students who are physically disabled, for example. In this school, I remind students that we are one school: we are not a rich school, we are not a posh school nor are we a school only for the physically able bodied. We are one school, a comprehensive school dedicated to serving the educational and social needs of all students, no matter their appearance, ability or background.
>
> Principal 5, England, male

The provision of free schools meals (FSMs) to students has been an established indicator of poverty among families/children in the UK for close to two decades and for just under a decade in Jamaica.

> The school's catchment area is very poor. The Parent Teachers' Association (PTA) runs an active breakfast club every morning for needy students and have done so for many years. Now that our most needy students have access [to] free lunches under the Programme for Advancement through Health & Education (PATH), many more students are being helped. Some students are a bit embarrassed to go [and] collect their free lunch however and we must continue to find ways to make it easier for them to do so. However, this PATH facility has made it easier for students to attend school and without the extra worry about 'lunch money'.
>
> Principal 3, Jamaica, female

We have over 300 students at school who are in receipt of free school meals. This is a high number. And that's why we have to ensure that these students are at school and learn so that they can turn things around for themselves and their families. Without question, the free school meals provision has gone a long way in driving down absenteeism, and I know in a small number of cases the meal the students receive at school is likely to be the only hot meal for the day.

                                                        Principal 9, England, female

The relationship between receiving an education and social mobility was recognized by principals from both Jamaica and England. Although formal state funded programmes may not be in place in developing countries, informal support programmes run by schools in partnership with community and parenting groups may exist, as they try to assist students from poorer families. But by themselves, breakfast feeding programmes and/or the provision of FSMs aren't enough. Principals also highlighted the plight of students who are unable to find the material and supplies they need for lessons, of some not being able to go on trips, and of others not wearing appropriate or required school uniform or being able to attend to their personal hygiene due to poverty-related issues. The relationship between poverty and social mobility has been widely debated by policy makers in both Jamaica and the UK, and despite interventions this relationship appears quite a strong one.

Positioning gender

Gender and schooling is an issue of ongoing debate in education in developed and developing countries. Issues of access, participation and outcomes have been documented, alongside class, ethnicity, cultural and religious issues. Recent reports on the MDGs (United Nations 2010, 2013) continue to highlight access to schooling as problematic. Whereas access, participation and achievement are improving for girls in nearly all countries, the achievement of boys lags behind (United Nations, 2010). Although access and participation in schooling among boys and girls alike in Jamaica and England may be described as areas of mild concern, achievement outcomes remain an area of serious concern which continues to attract national and international attention. For example, in 2014, the World Economic Forum's Insight Report placed the UK 32nd and Jamaica 37th, on a global list, in terms of educational attainment based on gender (WEF, 2014).

In 2007, the UK's Department for Education and Skills (DfES, 2007) reported there was no clear evidence of the impact of single-sex schooling on educational attainment. It also found the attitude of girls and boys towards certain subjects was influenced by whether they attended. No principal in this case study was in charge of a single-sex school. However, the issue of having the right mix of staff was important to them.

> We are very clear that, as a co-educational institution, we have to have a good mix of staff in terms of gender. Recently we appointed a male teacher for religious studies, bringing to three the number of teachers in that department. We would have been pleased to appoint a female if she had been the better candidate; but in a sense both were equally good and we went for the male since there are already two female teachers in that department.
>
> Principal 9, female

The achievement of boys remains an area of concern for principals. Although there was increasing evidence this had improved in recent years (DfES, 2007), English principals, especially, believed there was more to be done in narrowing the gender attainment gap, with some principals describing school-based initiatives they had used to secure improvements in this area.

> We recognize the issue of boys' underachievement is trending down, but we cannot pretend that the current situation is acceptable either. We regularly review our provision to all students so as to ensure we are adequately catering to their learning needs and their learning styles. What started off in 2008 as a six member Working Group on Boys Achievement has grown into an embedded part of our whole school reflective practice: so we look at the achievement of boys in general, boys with disabilities, boys from working-class backgrounds and boys from different ethnic groups. Our intention is that we raise the prospects for our students through reviews of subjects offered and the extracurricular activities we provide. We are keen that no student is left behind, but we do recognize that boys' achievement, although improving, remains a problem for us.
>
> Principal 6, England, male

Although acknowledging girls' performance in national tests continued to surpass that of boys, the overall patterns of participation and outcomes among both girls and boys were considered equally important.

> Girls' and boys' participation in education is about equal in this school, and a similar pattern may be found to exist across the country as a whole. Girls still outperform boys in national examinations and this remains a challenge.

> I think it's good that enrolment at primary school is almost 100 per cent but as a country we have to ensure that outcomes for students increase with increased participation.
>
> Principal 4, Jamaica, female

Gender and staffing did not escape the attention of principals. In England, there are marked gender differences in the school workforce. There are more female teachers at nursery, primary and secondary levels although men are more likely to get promoted as principals. In 2007 the DfES suggested 'the gender mix of teachers could play a role in the observed gender gap in attainment but this is difficult to measure and there is no strong evidence to date that this is the case' (DfES, 2007, p. 12). As with the UK, the gender mix of staff in schools in Jamaica is similarly problematic. In 2012, Ministry of Education data confirmed there were more female teachers at the nursery, primary and secondary levels (MoE, 2012). Differences between male and female principals had been set out in a number of research studies (Carli & Eagly, 2011; Eagly & Carli, 2007), although with results that were mixed. To date, and despite the patterns of difference no hard evidence exists to suggest that female principals are more or less effective than male principals and are indeed consistently different in traits and behaviours compared to male principals (van Engen et al., 2001). What is relatively certain however is the continuing glass ceiling that many female principals face in their career, often due to child-bearing and child-rearing, as well as due to dominant sociocultural structures and strictures within organizations and countries (Schedlitzki & Edwards, 2014).

Positioning multiculturalism

It is likely that many schools in large cities in both developed and developing countries, given the pace and spread of globalization, might be expected to be 'multicultural'. Multiculturalism involves *acknowledging* the validity of the cultural expressions and contributions of different groups (Wright et al., 2012). It also means *valuing* what people have to offer, and not rejecting or belittling it simply because it differs from what the majority, or those in power, regard as important and valuable (Race, 2013). At this time of globalization, cultural pluralism and increased frequency of contact between people of different cultures, effective leadership of multiculturalism is a necessary prerequisite for successful organizations, be they schools or otherwise (Yukl, 2012). Although there is no formal theory of global leadership, there are several ways in which culture impacts leadership (Daft, 2011).

School leaders need to develop cross-cultural competencies. In other words, whether a school principal, for example, is operating 'at home' or 'abroad', he/she will invariably come into increased contact with persons from different parts of the world and will need to 'engage with' and 'respond to' them appropriately. Adler and Bartholomew (1992) propose five essential skills a leader needs in order to successfully operate in a multicultural environment. First, leaders need to understand the business, political and cultural environments worldwide. Second, leaders should learn to understand the perspectives, tastes, trends and technologies of many other cultures. Third, they need to learn to work with people from different cultures. Fourth, they should be able to adapt to living and communicating in other cultures. Fifth, leaders need to learn to relate to people from other cultures from a position of equality, rather than a position of cultural superiority.

> I would describe my school as being truly multicultural and inclusive. We embrace all nationalities and cultures. We cannot be in twenty-first century Britain and be ignorant about who our neighbours are and their lifestyles. Our students need to understand the meaning of multiculturalism.
>
> Principal 5, England, male

A principal's role is vital to getting students to *acknowledge* and *value* 'otherness' and 'difference' in multicultural education and activities delivered at school in different ways. In this case study, principals described several different approaches used by their schools in trying to build and enhance cross-cultural understanding among staff and students. The actions of some principals and political actors in promoting intercultural awareness and dialogue would seemingly be met with approval from Race and Lander (2014) who identify a narrative of deficit among some political leaders in England, in relation to how 'others' are positioned.

Spotlight 8: Leading in diversity

Inner London Primary England is led by Dave* who is in his mid- to late forties. This is his second appointment as a principal and he has been in his current post for one year. He has a doctoral qualification in education. He also has international teaching experience, having previously taught in Australia. Inner London

Primary England has approximately 60 staff comprising 40 teachers including Dave and one deputy headteacher (male). There are approximately 430 students on roll who are taught in year groups from 1 to 6. Inner London Primary England also has a nursery attached to it, although physically located on the adjoining property. Dave is also in charge of the nursery that is managed on a day-to-day basis by a nursery manager. Inner London Primary is a publicly funded school run by the Catholic Church.

The school has modern amenities and facilities including a new computer laboratory. It is located in a 'safe' enclave of a 'deprived' community and is in close proximity to the stadium owned and operated by a popular football club. Students at Inner London Primary England usually make a successful transition to nearby secondary schools. They come from homes with different characteristics. For example, some are from homes where one or more parents work. Others are from homes where no parent works. Many children are from homes headed by a single parent. There are no physically disabled students at the school although many have a statement of special educational needs due to having a diagnosis of attention deficit hyperactivity disorder (ADHD).

There are more boys at the school than girls and students are from approximately 30 different nationalities, speaking over 30 different languages. Dave prides himself as leading 'a multicultural' and 'inclusive' school that values each student and staff member equally. He cites numerous examples of organizing 'international evenings', 'culture days' and 'themed weeks' where the different world cultures represented by staff and students are engaged with and celebrated. Dave describes these events as 'successful' and at times also involving the local community.

At Inner London Primary England, pictures and posters in different languages are mounted on walls and boards around the school. In addition, there are also flags mounted around the school that say to the community 'we are open for business' and shows the students that 'we value you'. The school also runs an 'open house' each term and 'coffee mornings' on the first Monday morning of each month. Parents and other community members are invited to 'drop in' and see what is done. These activities and events affirm staff and students and their own cultural and ethnic identities.

Doing multiculturalism

Principals shared the steps they took in trying to expand the cultural horizons of students through activities aimed at developing and promoting cultural awareness and understanding throughout the school. The influence of globalization and the 'shifting borderland narrative' (Miller, 2012, p. 9) led to them taking active steps to engage with and inform students and staff about 'others' around them.

> We have pupils from over 35 nationalities at school. We have a day set aside for internationalism where we encourage pupils and their families to get involved with the school through sharing their culture – food, music, art and dance. Our teachers and pupils benefit from this kind of exposure tremendously since it helps to promote understanding and build school/parent/community relations.
>
> Principal 5, England, male

Informal CPD opportunities were recognized as having the potential to provide staff with better and more reliable information not found in textbooks, thereby allowing and enabling them to draw more authoritative comparisons and conclusions and to provide students with more and better examples when teaching.

> Part of our mission is to prepare pupils to become global citizens. As a result, we actively engage with other cultures and other educational systems. To be honest, some colleagues 'don't get' why we'd fly halfway across the world to country X or country Y when we have nationals from these countries living and working in our country. But the governors and I feel it is critical for our school to not only say it prepares pupils to be global citizens but to, as far as possible, support staff and pupils in building their understanding of each other and in deepening the intercultural dialogue in a way you will never be able to get from reading a book or from simply hearing stories about a place.
>
> Principal 1, England, male

Based on their study on *North South School Partnerships*, Edge et al. (2009) reported that UK schools benefited from these partnerships in terms of content and context knowledge, whereas aspirations and outcomes among students were boosted for students in Africa and Asia.

International partnerships

Although not being able to fund a trip abroad for students, some principals envisioned being able to do so, in order to expose students to a worldly mindset (Wenger, 1991).

> We would love to be able to take our students and teachers overseas to give them exposure to another culture, another country. The issue for us is that we do not

have good and credible contacts overseas and we also do not have the money to fund a trip abroad. But we are well aware that our students, in a sense, are living [in] a television and internet bubble which may not always accurately represent another country and culture. If we can find a partner and the funds, we'd go visit another country; and if we can't find the funds to physically visit but can find the money to build the infrastructure for virtual partnerships between our school and others in another country, we would do that. We want our students to be well exposed.

Principal 8, Jamaica, female

Principals reported that not everyone in a school community readily provides support to international partnership working and/or actual participating in international visits and exchanges:

Some of my teachers have told me, 'The pupils suffer when they go abroad on trips. They fall behind in their work . . . they find it difficult to catch up . . . and it creates extra work for them in trying to support those learners'. I am sure they are right in some cases, but I always say to them, 'We are here for the pupils . . . to provide them [with] the best educational opportunities and experience'. It's difficult to get staff to support international school partnerships sometimes – not because they can't see the added value to be gained but because they worry about their workload.

Principal 9, England, female

One principal was however resolute that international partnerships work to the benefit of schools and should be promoted and supported more widely:

I have heard it said that these partnerships create opportunities for certain people to travel abroad. My response to that is, 'Come and join me so you can go next time and I can stay and run the school'. Unfortunately there are colleagues who sit on the fence and criticize, citing the costs of trips and how exclusive it will be, but they never get involved. But we've taken pupils abroad who have contributed zero towards their airfare or accommodation because they simply could not afford to pay. So it's not about the money. Far from opportunities being created for some people to travel, I am creating opportunities for our school and pupils to 'reach out' and for our students to deepen their understanding of the human condition.

Principal 6, England, male

Principals who had themselves participated in international visits felt strongly that these were 'life changing' and benefited entire school communities, not only those who participated directly. Of partnerships, the UK's former schools minister, David Miliband (2003), suggested they 'expand the horizons of young people, and ensures that their progress inside the classroom is supported outside it. Partnerships are challenging but they are also exciting. They require brokerage, planning and critical review' (p. 3). More broadly, he suggested partnerships could contribute to more effective teaching and learning, lead to a more 'informed professionalism' and the ability of professionals in schools to lead change, and offer real opportunities for schools to get involved in multi-agency working and cross-cultural learning.

Principals were all agreed that setting up partnerships of any kind required time and focus. They also agreed that, if carefully conceptualized from the start, and closely monitored at every stage, partnership working, especially partnerships between institutions in different countries, can be beneficial. They were clear that despite challenges involved in setting up, managing and sustaining partnerships, partnership working offered an entire school community, students and teachers especially, an opportunity to deepen, broaden and extend learning and teaching in many areas and on many topics, and in many ways that textbooks alone and/ or the Internet are unable to provide. This mirrored findings from recent and ongoing research on whole-school capacity-building through study tours (Miller & Potter, 2014).

Spotlight 9: Study tours

At least three principals had been directly involved in international study tours. They saw study tours as an important form of capacity-building that not only 'added to staff and students' but also to their own intercultural capacities and understanding. Two principals had participated in study tours to Europe, including England, whereas one had participated in study tours to the Caribbean and Africa. They each described individual, interpersonal and whole-school learning derived from their participation in international study tours, such as developing a sense of greater knowledge and understanding of peoples, places and cultures in other parts of the world. Knowledge and other gains in learning did not always leave principals excited or happy but rather 'perplexed' due to the poverty and in 'awe' and 'admiration' due to the commitment, creativity and resilience shown by both teachers and principals – especially those in developing countries. This 'duality of emotions' led to a view among principals that these visits helped to 'put things into perspective' and to become 'annoyed' with much of the 'wastage of resources that goes on in our schools' and 'the things we take for granted'.

Positioning social justice and schooling

The issues presented and discussed so far in this chapter lead us to a discussion on social justice. Without question, principals across the world are being confronted by the ever increasing diversity of schools. There are schools that select students on the basis of their family income, ability or faith; there are also schools that specialize in certain areas of the curriculum (such as sport, science or languages), and in England some state-funded schools are allowed to operate outside of the control of local (education) authorities (Miller, 2011). Another feature of current education systems is the vocabulary used to describe the shortcomings of schools, teachers and students. For example, in England, over the last 20 years or so, much has been written about 'sink schools' and 'bog standard comprehensives', populated mostly by students from working-class families, while the affluent and (more) able have been 'creamed off' to other, more selective schools (Smith, 2012, p. 7). In Jamaica, however, the narrative is usually framed in terms of upgraded high schools versus traditional high schools where upgraded high schools (or comprehensives) are considered 'not as good' and where traditional high schools do better because they get the more affluent and more able students (Hutton, 2011).

Much has also been written about schools being 'named and shamed' and described as 'failing' or having been placed in 'special measures' where 'leadership is poor' and where teachers are believed to be 'useless' (Smith, 2012, p. 11). But all schools are not the same and those that operate in wealthier areas with a more 'well off' student population are more likely to do better. Similarly, those that have a larger network of benefactors are more likely to receive extra support than those which do not. All schools are not the same and all students' school experiences are not equal. Whereas this fact is well recognized by principals, it is sometimes debatable, even among principals, as to whether policy-makers, parents and the public at large acknowledge these differences since the role of education in promoting equality and social justice has been a major preoccupation of politicians who play a central role in deciding what is taught in our schools, where it is taught, to whom and by whom (Hill & Cole, 2001). In other words, governments in both developed and developing countries tend to regard education as the engine of social mobility and economic growth, although Woolf (2000) has argued that 'our preoccupation with education as an engine of growth has ... narrowed – dismally and progressively – our vision of education itself' (p. 254). Nevertheless, as proposed by Brighouse (2006), 'the central purpose of education is to promote human flourishing' (p. 42) which is consistent with the overlapping themes of the UDHR as discussed earlier in this chapter.

The policies that schools implement, and as a result that get played out in schools (e.g. what curriculum to study), have emerged from different political views on how best to achieve an education system suited to the current and future needs and demands of society: 'Without good education there can be no social justice' (Cameron, 2007); 'It is education which provides the rungs on the ladder of social mobility' (Brown, 2010). The role of education in reducing inequality and promoting social mobility is an important topic among politicians, even from opposing parties, who agree that schools, as socializing agents, and what gets taught in them, are important to promoting social justice. According Brighouse (2006), schools 'should orient themselves to the needs of the children who will have to deal with the economy, and not to the needs of the economy itself' (p. 28). He further highlights that the education provided at schools should enable students to:

- become 'autonomous, self-governing adults' (p. 131);
- become economically self-reliant;
- 'lead flourishing lives' (p. 42);
- become 'responsible, deliberative citizens who are capable of accepting the demands of justice and abiding by the norm of reciprocity' (p. 131).

The view that education, and therefore schooling, has a central role in encouraging students to lead flourishing lives emphasizes the critical role of schools and that of principals. As discussed elsewhere in this chapter, schools are microcosms of society. And as Haber (2009) suggests, schools can be problematic spaces that perpetuate and reproduce inequalities through practices and activities considered to be oppressive, dominative, indoctrinating, deferential, docile, institutionalized, taming and controlling. Haber's views are not without controversy; yet, all the more underlining the critical role of school leader(ship) in ensuring all students at school, regardless of gender, race/ethnicity, social class and/or any other characteristics, are treated with fairness, justice, inclusivity, respect and equality. The role of an education department or ministry in providing ongoing support to schools and principals cannot be overlooked. In the words of former British Prime Minister Gordon Brown, 'fairness can be advanced but cannot, in the end, be guaranteed by charities, however benevolent, by markets, however dynamic, or by individuals, however well meaning, but guaranteed only by [an] enabling government' (Brown 2005).

Reflection

Respect, fairness, equality and justice are examples of important values to be found in professional codes of conduct for teachers and principals and also in school curricula around the world. Principals have a major role in the creation and promotion of social harmony and democracy in society, through personal leadership examples, and through activities and events delivered at school, and based on how the curriculum is presented to students. Principals (and teachers) have a role to play in curtailing discourses of deficit and hate directed towards any member of society, be they members of a school community or not. Schools cannot pretend to be inclusive or pretend to practise inclusion. Rather, they must practise inclusion and been seen to do so, from the principal's office to the lunchroom, the staffroom and to the classroom. There can be no excuses.

The importance of multiculturalism, as Triandafyllidou et al. (2012) argue in Europe, focuses on 'the political accommodation by the state and/or a dominant group' (p. 5). For a school principal, however, multiculturalism must move beyond political accommodation to contextual enactment. According to Race and Lander (2014), this however requires a 're-think to be carried out in both staffrooms and classrooms' (p. 213) in order to avoid stereotypical perceptions and in order to move towards what Dolby (2012) calls a 'new multiculturalism' in which teachers, students, families and school leaders also actively engage with cross-cultural and intercultural learning opportunities.

Learning with and about each other has to be foundational to a curriculum delivered to students in the twenty-first century. Whereas principals are not responsible for the content of the curriculum, they nonetheless can influence what gets put into it. In other words, principals can recommend and/or lobby for changes to curriculum subjects (e.g. in England, citizenship and in Jamaica, civics), to more closely reflect the shared similarities and experiences of diverse peoples who live, work and study together. And while in pursuit of opportunities to deepen the learning experience for students and/or building a school's intercultural outreach, it is important that principals seek to include and integrate multiple interests into a single coherent narrative that tells a story of what a school is about – thereby limiting the chances of being branded 'exclusive' and/or 'discriminatory'.

4

Technology Leadership

All the students we teach have something in their lives that's really engaging – something that they do and that they are good at, something that has an engaging, creative component to it. Some may download songs; some may rap, lip sync, or sing karaoke; some may play video games; some may mix songs; some may make movies; and some may do the extreme sports that are possible with twenty-first-century equipment and materials. But they all do something engaging.

Prensky, 2005, p. 62

As technology use and costs have soared, school leaders have more pressure to manage and monitor the investment. Principals don't have to be technology experts to lead their school toward effective technology use, but they do need to be informed.

Gosmire & Grady, 2007, p. 1

Introduction

There can be no doubt that information and communication technology (ICT) plays an important part in supporting education and training at all levels of an education system. From teaching and learning to budgeting, procurement, recording of incidents, registering attendance and communicating within and outside school, the use of technology is foundational to schools' efficiency and to the 'experience' of those who study and work in them. These are but a few basic scenarios that illustrate the need for further use and integration of ICT into everyday school processes. Around the world, data management systems are being used to enable education ministries and/or departments, and individual schools, to use data to improve education and meet policy demand, although in some developing countries, especially, this has been found not to be the case (Dzidonu, 2010).

According to Farrell (2007), advances in technologies are making it easier for educational providers to develop and provide educational and training programmes at all levels of national educational systems in countries around the world. In addition, the introduction and integration of ICT to support teaching and learning and the administration of education at the school, district, zone, region or national level is profoundly changing the delivery of education and the support landscape available to schools and other educational institutions across the world. In other words, the integration and use of ICT in the processes of a school can lead to benefits for all who study and work therein. For example, an education ministry and/or an examination authority may wish to share large amounts of data, simultaneously, with schools located in different parts of a country. A school may have to be closed unexpectedly and students still have to be 'taught' during this physical time away from campus. A parent may wish to find out what his or her child's tasks and/or grades are in a specific class. A student may need to download class notes or a year group leader may want to send an important message to all students on a specific topic or issue.

The important role of technology in supporting the delivery of education and training, in multiple ways, cannot be overstated. Education ministries and/or departments and school leaders are giving more and more attention to technological issues and how these relate to the *design, development, delivery* and *distribution* of educational programmes, whether through a virtual format or face to face. Not only does this acknowledge differences in learners, it suggests principals understand the learners in their schools and are prepared to create conditions for supporting teaching and learning in and through technology (Gosmire & Grady, 2007).

Student achievement and technology is problematic. A number of reasons have been put forward for this including emphasis on standards-based accountability (Whitehead et al., 2003), insufficient investment in financial and human resources in purchasing and implementing technology (Brockmeier et al., 2005), inadequate engagement among principals (Nance, 2003), the digital divide (Prensky, 2005), infrastructure issues (Warschauer et al., 2004) and issues of digital equity and lack of computer access at home (Watson, 2013). As a result, the technology has not yielded the anticipated student achievement outcomes (Whitehead et al., 2003).

Nevertheless, as Dzidonu (2010) surmises, 'the explosive growth in network technologies and products and the rapid spread of the Internet, as well as the advances in multimedia and collaborative software environment is fueling a new wave of better teaching, training and learning tools' (p. 5). Put differently, technology is fuelling opportunities for schools and for students, although Nance (2003) has observed that principals are only moderately involved in technology planning and policy-making. If what Dzidonu says is correct, then the integration and (extensive) use of educational technologies in schools promises more than just improvements in educational productivity, requiring principals to take the leadership in advocacy, procurement, design, development and delivery, and as a result provide teachers and students with a qualitatively different teaching and learning experience in and through technology.

Vision and technology leadership

Technology leadership is an important part of a principal's leadership. The principal must establish the vision and goals for technology in a school. He or she carries the vision 'banner' and promotes the vision throughout the school (Grady, 2011a, 2011b). Principals and teachers need a technology-supported pedagogical knowledge and skills base which they can draw on when integrating technology into school functions and classroom instruction (Hughes, 2013).

As the leader, a principal is responsible for establishing a context for use and integration of technology in their school and understanding how technology can be used to redefine learning environments and experiences and empower teachers and students. It is the principal's role to establish a vision for the school. Principals must establish a context for technology in the school and set out or clarify how the technology can be used to restructure learning, empower teachers and help students become more technology literate (Brockmeier et al., 2005). In other words, a principal is *the key* to efforts and attempts towards integrating technology into teaching and learning activities and, where possible, into other processes. Lack of visionary leadership has been found to be a major reason for schools not being important players in the information age (Bailey, 1997). Principals must use their 'leadership to step up the pace, and create [a] sense of urgency, vision and strategic plan' (Grady, 2011a, p. 4). The vision could include:

- the leadership the principal exerts on technology integration into teaching and learning and other processes;
- the role of teachers in integrating technology into teaching and learning activities;
- the standards to be used to guide the technology plan for the school;
- the measures that will be applied to assess technology use;

- the resources that are necessary to enable effective use of technology by students and teachers, showcasing the use of technology to facilitate student learning and achievement.

Recent research from the Caribbean shows that, in addition to a principal's role in introducing and using ICT, there still exists a digital divide between teachers and students (Watson, 2013). The vision of how and why technology is to be used in schools is critical to identifying what a school is going to do with technology, how it is going to reach its goals and how technology can help to narrow the digital gap that exists between teachers and students. Lawton (2010, p. 70) found three challenges that can potentially undermine efforts by principals to integrate ICT at school:

- insufficient access to ICT equipment and resources;
- a curriculum that focuses on examination preparations and basic technology skills rather than on the application of technology to develop critical thinking and higher-value skills (which restricts the embedding of ICT use in teaching and learning);
- insufficient capacity both in terms of adequately trained teachers and institutional capacity to implement policies.

These challenges aside, preparing students to live independently in a digital world can only result from informed, creative, instructional leadership that is transformative and forward-thinking and that is directed towards change for both the individual learner and for society as a whole. Hope and Stakenas (1999) proposed three roles for the principal as technology leader: role model, instructional leader and visionary. In other words, they must 'know enough' about specific technology tools – such as email, databases, the Internet, word processing and simple spreadsheets – in order to demonstrate the use of technology for administrative and managerial tasks. Importantly, principals who make technology a routine part of their jobs provide an example and a commitment that can help others acquire technology expertise (Brockmeier et al., 2005).

A principal's leadership of technology use aside however, a number of other key ingredients are required for the effective and seamless implementation, integration and use of technology in schools. These include:

- a national policy that drives ICT and sets out the overarching vision;
- integration of ICT into the curriculum being delivered to trainee teachers so they are equipped with both content and skills;
- the physical infrastructure and resources that support quality provision;

- a school-level policy that derives its purpose from and supports national policy;
- appropriately trained staff, at all levels.

Technology leadership involves understanding the role and impact of technology on society and individuals, accepting responsibility for living in a technologically oriented information age and using technology as a tool for obtaining, organizing and manipulating information for communication and creative expression (Afshari et al., 2009). Schools are changing rapidly and so are the demands and expectations of students. As principals come to terms with changes in school populations, class sizes, ethnic, gender and social class demographics, and the range and choice of subjects offered to students, they are also confronted by rapid changes in the technology being used, which is forcing them to consider the composite capacity of their schools to provide students with an educational experience that is appropriate to their needs.

Spotlight 10: Remote Primary One Jamaica – technology leadership

Remote Primary One is led by Jane* who is in her late thirties. This is her first appointment as a principal and she has been in post for eight years. She has a master's degree in educational leadership & management. Remote Primary One has four teachers, including Jane. There are 75 students on roll who are taught in 'multi-grades' (grades 1 and 2 together; grades 3 and 4 together; and grades 5 and 6 on their own). The school has one ancillary member of staff who doubles as 'cook' and 'cleaner'. There is also a 'watchman'. Jane does not have a secretary or administrative assistant.

The school has one outside toilet for staff and two outside toilets for students (one each for girls and boys). It is located in a remote part of Jamaica where some people still bathe in the river and where students 'carry water for cooking and drinking on their heads' from a nearby standpipe. Many parents of students at Remote Primary One do not work and the majority of those who do are farmers, working within the local community.

Jane wants her students to be 'exposed' to the world 'outside their village' and to be given as many skills (including social skills) as possible for when they move outside the village for, for example, to secondary schooling.

Jane calls a meeting of the parents and community leaders. Nearly all parents turn up. In Jane's words, 'most parents can't read and write, but they all place a high value on education and want their children to achieve a better station in life'. At the meeting Jane discusses plans to purchase four computers. The parents are excited and hooked. They like the idea although they do not have much to contribute financially to the project. Together, Jane and a group of parents organize a series of community events (film shows, school fayres, etc.) and after six months, and with some sponsorship from the community, they are able to purchase three computers.

The school does not have internet access but it does have electricity. For Jane, teachers, parents and students, the purchase of the computers is an important achievement that 'opens up a new world for these children'. Jane will be the computer teacher as none of the other teachers are skilled enough to take on this role.

Principals' use of ICT

Principals in this study fully grasped the importance of and urgent need to integrate ICT into school processes and teaching and learning activities. They were resolved that they have an important role to play in getting students exposed or introduced to ICT at school despite the rapidly changing technological environment. Nevertheless, their own use of ICT and their ability to use it is often an important consideration in the drive to outfit a school and classrooms with ICT facilities. The importance of principals' ICT literacy and competence has been highlighted by Gosmire & Grady (2007) who point out that a principal's technology skills should involve learning how to operate technology and using it whenever possible for carrying out their own duties, especially when communicating with others.

> I am fairly competent in the use of ICT. In fact, I have been using computers in my work for over 20 years and they make things so much easier and quicker. That's partly why I pressed the governors and local authority for us to provide each teacher with a laptop, so that they can use it in every possible aspect of their teaching and learning and other work-related roles . . . and we've kitted them out with all kinds of software to do just that.
>
> Principal 9, England, female

The paradox of this statement was widely shared by principals in terms of their own skills and capacity, the availability of financial and other resources and staff skills and capacity. The Jamaican principals faced more severe resource constraints compared with English principals since Jamaican schools are only part subsidised by the government, and in some cases many operated without computers. Those with computers sometimes did not have enough or even electricity to power them. Returning to the paradox of ICT skills and capacity however, Awalt and Jolly (1999) suggest that a reason for the lack of informed leadership in technology 'has been the struggle to identify the "administrator knowledge base" needed in technology and the management of technology in the school situation' (p. 4). This is an interesting proposal operating at two levels, both in terms of whole-school processes and also at the level of teaching and learning.

> I must admit, I am slow off the mark with the use of ICTs as I am an older person. Having said that, I am now attending classes to build my capacity, so when I talk to staff about integrating ICT in their teaching, I don't feel hypocritical about it and I can do so being able to assist someone who is unsure.
>
> Principal 8, Jamaica, female

Among principals was a conviction that they needed to be and become 'role models as technology users and supporters for students, teachers, and support staff' (Heaton & Washington, 1999, p. 4). This was built on the premise that they need to model the use of technology in order to change and improve the environment in which teachers and students operate ... leading to a climate in which the use of ICTs is viewed 'as an attribute of schools rather than an attribute of individuals' (Anderson & Dexter, 2005, p. 53). In being able to practise their vision for ICT integration, they were leading from the front, sending a powerful message through both words and actions (Flanagan & Jacobsen, 2003).

Spotlight 11: English schools and ICT

On balance, schools in England are reasonably well resourced in terms of their ICT infrastructure. Although English principals agreed that their schools could have more facilities such as more computer laboratories, they all described what they have available as 'adequate for the numbers [of students] we have'. In addition, all English schools in this case study operate a functional virtual learning environment (VLE), thereby providing students additional opportunities to extend their use of and engagement with ICT from home.

At least two English principals expressed a degree of concern about some 'older' teachers who did not integrate ICT into their teaching and learning and about some younger teachers whose integration of ICT was 'superficial' and usually limited to the use of PowerPoint. On the whole however, these principals pointed to staff who were using ICT in their classrooms 'to stimulate interest in learning' and 'to improve teaching processes', among whom were some teachers for whom this integration was 'natural'.

Some teachers find it a bit daunting to incorporate the use of ICT into their lessons. Yet many have done so with great success. Although there is no blueprint for getting started, we tell our teachers to strive to provide students with the best educational experience. We tell them, 'learn along with the students . . . but don't deny them the best learning experience . . .'

Principal 2, England, female

Principals stated their commitment to providing additional support for teachers in the form of training, usually undertaken at the end of a school day with an ICT teacher or through external providers contracted by schools to provide this service. However, they also cited examples of some teachers 'making every possible excuse not to attend' and 'not to incorporate technology in their teaching due being overly self-conscious'. The leadership and pedagogical implications are clear.

Teachers and ICT

Teachers are integral to the provision and delivery of ICT to students. Through their skills, experience, enthusiasm and example, they model the use of technology into teaching and learning. Despite efforts by some governments to provide technology-driven education (Ullman, 2013) and despite efforts by many principals to embed the use of technology in schools (Chin, 2010), many schools have been unable to successfully do so, for reasons connected to teachers, who are expected to play a central role in leading the delivery of knowledge and skills development among students. Livingston and Wirt (2005) reported several 'issues' that presented challenges to teachers' buying into and therefore using and/or supporting the use of ICT at school:

- attitudes and beliefs about how much time is required to integrate technology in the classroom;
- proficiency level, as some feel unprepared and unaware of the content-based practices that the Internet has to offer;
- lack of confidence in how to integrate technology into their instructional practices due to inadequate professional development;
- lack of continuity and follow-up through CPD.

Principals shared similar reflections:

Most of our learners have computers at home . . . and some are far more advanced in the use of ICTs than their teachers. We realize this can hamper teaching and learning and as a result we provide all teachers with regular CPD opportunities for them to build their ICT profile. We cannot afford for our kids to be left behind.

Principal 9, England, female

Although as a school we emphasize that teachers make use of digital technologies in teaching and learning, we have teachers on staff who are a bit 'apprehensive' about using ICT in lessons. Teachers who understand the technology will use it to their advantage, but those who do not understand or prefer to cling to a bygone era, require a bit more support . . . and as a leadership team, we are aware of who those teachers are . . .

Principal 2, England, female

As noted earlier in this chapter, principals have a central role in determining if, when and how well technology is utilized in their schools. And in order for students to be exposed to and use technology to its full potential they rely on the vision of principals and on the knowledge, skills and support of teachers. But teacher capacity is a major factor in the successful provision and delivery of effective ICT provision in schools (Lai & Pratt, 2004), with implications for educational systems and schools around the world. Fear could severely undermine teachers' engagement with and therefore efficacy in using technology, whether they are experienced or not. And it is the principal's responsibility to understand the cause of that fear, defuse it and get teachers to support their vision and provide students with richer and better opportunities for learning. Supporting teacher professional development in ICT is therefore an urgent requirement for twenty-first century schools (Grady, 2011a) since this is essential to enhancing the skills of teachers, staff and students and for achieving the vision and goals of a school (Grady, 2011b).

Students and ICT

Principals are required to lead in a way that promote the best interest of all students. In the global digital era, this becomes a more fundamental requirement for schools. The UNCRC (1989) affirms a child's 'right to education' (Article 28). Article 29a requires governments and/or agencies acting on behalf of a government to ensure the education a child receives is directed towards 'the development of the child's personality, talents and mental and physical abilities to their fullest potential'. Article 29a is supplemented by Article 13(1) which states: 'The child shall have the right to freedom of expression; this right shall include freedom to seek, receive and impart information and ideas of all kinds, regardless of frontiers, either orally, in writing or in print, in the form of art, or through any other media of the child's choice.' Given this position, set out in international law, principals, on these bases, are inclined to do all they can so that their students can be provided with the 'best' educational experience possible. Invariably, for the times we live in, this would include training in the *appreciation*, understanding and use of technology. Although some schools have no or only limited access to ICT facilities and resources, and although some do not have suitably trained and qualified staff, the principals in this case study were acutely aware of how ICT can impact the learning experience of students. In addition, they were also aware of the importance of students having appropriate skills in ICT:

> Last year I launched a six-month fundraising campaign for the school. My aim was to get four computers so that students in grades five and six could get an 'introduction to computing' before going to high school. They need this exposure. My school is located in a deep rural community and access to computers and internet at home is rather limited. The fundraising campaign raised enough money to purchase three computers which I now use to teach the kids. I am not an ICT teacher but I do the best I can as we can't afford to employ a specialist ICT teacher.
>
> Principal 4, Jamaica, female

In a speech to launch the report *Unseen Children: Access and achievement 20 years on* (Ofsted, 2013), HMCI Sir Michael Wilshaw described some students in rural England as the 'hidden' poor, lamenting the fact that, based on their location, they were denied access to the best available resources at school – sometimes, including subjects taught and quality of teachers. Whereas there is no denying the challenges faced by principals and schools in delivering an effective ICT provision to students, no two principals encountered the same challenges:

> We have a fairly well developed ICT provision at my school with three fully furnished computer laboratories. We have about 85 computers and students use the computer labs on a rotation system. We also have a fairly good VLE which our students use on a daily basis. Teachers are always updating the VLE with new content which we use to supplement on-site teaching and learning. We've successfully used the VLE in cases where students couldn't come into school due to heavy snow.
>
> Principal 5, England, male

Each principal told a different story about ICT at their school: the challenges, the issues, teachers' abilities, students' abilities, their own abilities and the differences among user groups within a school:

> There are five visually impaired students at school. We've received assistance from the local authority in modifying and purchasing specialist teaching and learning software. In addition, our ICT lead teacher has sourced ... specially adjusted hardware that can be used at school and at home. We've purchased these for our students so they are in the best possible position to do well and we, as a school, are in the best possible position to meet the needs of our disabled learners.
>
> Principal 9, England, female

> ICT is a good way to involve and include 'low ability learners'. Not only is teaching with ICT providing a different kind of learning experience for them, it's also motivating. Since many students have some form of access to some technology at home, our teachers have found that 'low ability learners' tend to 'spark' much more during these 'tactile' lessons since they get to 'show how much they know'. It's not always easy but we have to try to reach all learners. If they don't leave with the knowledge, then at least the skills they already have can be further enhanced.
>
> Principal 1, England, male

Undoubtedly principals know and understand that students who are taught in technology supported classrooms are afforded very powerful tools to help them gather and share information, and to network, providing them with increased awareness and confidence so they rely less on their teachers and more on their own initiative for knowledge creation and skills-building. ICT in education enables students to use information in a manner that accelerates their understanding and higher-order thinking skills (Tan, 2010). As we are reminded by Prensky (2010), 'Students want to learn differently than in the past ... The key change and challenge for all 21st century teachers is to become comfortable not with the details of new technology, but rather with a different and better kind of pedagogy ...' (p. 3).

School processes and ICT

In order to leverage the effects and impacts of ICT more widely throughout a school, and in order to improve overall efficiency, principals considered and integrated technology into other school processes, beyond teaching and learning:

We've recently computerized all our budgeting, procurement and accounting processes and this has made life easier for the school business manager (bursar) and her team. It's now much easier to complete procurement processes and to track items. Not only does it save time and money, the new computerized system also provides quick access to important details.

Principal 1, England, male

For quite some time we were plagued with petty theft, fighting, and all sorts of antisocial behaviour. About a year ago we introduced some CCTV cameras and they've gone some way in deterring students from behaving badly. Recently, one student stole a teacher's mobile phone from her handbag and flat out denied it. But CCTV showed him doing it – in the ICT lab!

Principal 5, England, male

All of our systems are computerized. Human resources, safety and security, including registering attendance. We even have a facility to send automated text messages to parents notifying them their child did not turn up to morning registration and is therefore not at school. And we have kitted out all our classrooms, including labs, with interactive whiteboards. The turnaround in some areas has been faster and greater than others, but overall it has simplified processes for everyone.

Principal 6, England, male

Technology can be a major catalyst for change and for more effective use of scarce resources. Effective technology leadership by principals is therefore contextualized in terms of what's possible and practical at *this point in time* in their schools, underpinned by environmental factors such as cost, sustainability, utility and advances in technology. Principals who are technologically literate are in a better position to determine the type of technology to introduce and implement in their schools and to evaluate whether the technology implemented has the potential to improve learning for all students (Ng, 2008).

ICT infrastructure

The challenges associated with the implementation and integration of ICT into a school's processes are not related only to principal and/or teacher capacity, attitudes, skills and beliefs. Effective ICT implementation and integration may also be hampered by inadequate, non-existent or outdated physical infrastructure. ICT infrastructure includes hardware, software and other resources. Hardware includes physical structure and equipment like computer networks, computers, projectors and printers. Software includes computer programs that can be used as generic tools to facilitate administration or learning – for example, learning management systems, spreadsheets or databases. Resources include information that could facilitate learning, such as a tutorial program or an online encyclopedia (Yee, 2000). From her study of ICT in Jamaican schools, Watson (2013, p. 150) reported:

> Jamaica is still at the stage where computers are still being introduced to the school system. Internet access is another important issue where a massive gap exists in Jamaica. For example, for the period December 2010 to 2011, the global figure for Internet users stood at 2,267,233,742, whereas the figure for the Caribbean was 11,893,504, and the figure for Jamaica was 1,581,100. There may be many reasons for this, for example, Jamaica's ICT infrastructure is not as advanced as the rest of the world, or many people may see having a computer as more important than having Internet access, or having a computer may not be seen as a priority when compared with basic necessities such as food.

Watson contrasts the ICT infrastructure available in Jamaican schools to that of schools in developed countries such as the United States and the United Kingdom:

> [P]eople in Jamaica may have a computer at home, but may not have the money to be able to afford Internet access. In the United Kingdom (UK) and the United States of America (USA), the majority of schools have integrated the use of Web 2.0 social networks into their ICT provision allowing students to communicate, upload and download files and create content.

The situation described by Watson in respect of Jamaica is not untypical of developing countries. Dzidonu (2010) reasons that despite the potential of ICT to transform teaching and learning and educational processes, there is a massive implementation gap in African countries, due almost entirely to economics. Nevertheless, principals surmised that inasmuch as economic conditions were a much talked about barrier to ICT implementation and integration, a country's or school's ICT infrastructure itself was a barrier that schools were finding increasingly difficult to ignore or accept:

> Our school buildings are quite old. To set up a proper ICT lab requires the laying of special cables which demand changes to the building itself. Given the state of some our school buildings, we would bet better off knocking down the existing buildings and building new ones. In the long run, this would be the cheaper option for schools. But based on the age of the buildings we have, and the state they are in, we cannot go drill into the walls and floors and put in the type of ICT infrastructure that is needed to support teaching and learning and administrative processes.
>
> Principal 4, Jamaica, female

Many of our [primary] schools do not have electricity in the classrooms. Electricity is connected to the main office and in the principal's office, but not usually in classrooms. To integrate ICT into learning and teaching means fixing these problems first. We want to make ICT routine in teaching and learning but the government and the business community has to help.

Principal 10, Jamaica, female

Although not all principals possessed the technical skills to model and lead the use of ICT at school, all were clear that students were living in an era that required schools to support students' technology scaffolding. Their efforts were however hampered, in many cases, by constraints outside their control and for which there were no quick fixes, which meant schools were left with two options: either to 'make do' and/or students 'doing without'.

Spotlight 12: Dilemmas and differences in ICT provision

There was a deep desire among all principals to provide students with the best possible educational experience. There were however some noticeable limitations and differences based on country contexts.

Principals in Jamaica did not have the facilities and equipment, and in some cases, neither did they have specialist ICT teachers on staff or within access. Nevertheless, what was clear among them was a concerted desire for their students to get access to new knowledge and new skills for use outside their immediate environments. And where they did not have specialist ICT teachers, existing teachers, even principals, would 'take the leadership' in trying to provide students with some knowledge and some skills. Where they did not have [adequate] facilities and equipment at their disposal, they would fundraise in order to try to provide these.

Principals in England however have a different set of challenges. Whereas they wanted more and better resources and equipment due to growing class sizes and due to swift changes in the technological environment, they were not confident students always received the best deal from teachers, despite schools having adequate resources to do so. In other words, although all English schools in this study have some ICT provision, teachers did not always make use of this provision in teaching and learning, and where use was made, sometimes, it was superficial. Additionally, where support was brought in to boost teachers' capacity and expertise, some teachers did not engage with this.

Implementing and integrating ICT

So far in this chapter, much attention has been given to principals, teachers and students. All of these should be ICT literate, and there are increasing individual, social and other benefits to this. Nevertheless, there are some other important issues and factors with which principals need to contend in order to be successful in integrating ICT at school. Based on studies of schools in Canada, New Zealand and the United States, Yee (2000, pp. 293–4) identified eight functional roles of the technology leader-principal:

- equitable provision of hardware and resources;
- learning-focused envisioning;
- adventurous learning (experimenting) with technologies;
- patient teaching (coaching) of teachers and students;
- protective enabling of teachers and students with shared leadership;
- constant monitoring of school progress;
- entrepreneurial networking with partners and stakeholders;
- careful challenging of staff to be innovative.

These roles are supplemented by Schiller (2002) who, based on studies conducted with school principals in Australia, found they had to assume and deploy different change strategies in order to successfully implement and integrate ICT at school:

- **Infrastructural change:** principals play a key role in providing adequate and suitable infrastructure that is conducive to the use of educational technologies at school. Within the constraints of what is possible, what is provided should be equitable to all staff and students, based on needs and school circumstances.
- **Organizational and policy change:** principals need to set up working groups and technology committees, seek external support, develop staff, safeguard available technological resources, budget for technology and appoint technology champions to help spread their vision (Anderson & Dexter, 2005).
- **Pedagogical and learning change:** learning and outcomes of learning should be linked to technology use and principals have to be prepared to show teachers the 'bigger picture' from their example through 'learning-focused envisioning' and 'adventurous learning' (Yee, 2000, p. 293). In other words,

while principals can build organization capacity through transformational leadership, the display of instructional leadership is more likely to enhance the individual competence of teachers and students.

- **Cultural change:** principals have to be consistent and constant about the use and integration of ICT. The way people perceive, think and feel about things in schools influences how they function (Maslowski, 2001; Tondeur et al., 2009). Although difficult to achieve, cultural change is arguably one of the most effective ways to achieve high quality and sustained integration of technology into classrooms (Yuen et al., 2003), but this requires that the use of ICT becomes the norm.

It is clear that the issues surrounding the integration of technology in schools are multifaceted, including individual, cultural, economic and infrastructural. It is of note however that despite the nature of the challenge or challenges facing a school, all principals were highly committed to providing students and staff with opportunities to develop what Prokopiadou (2012) calls 'critical ICT awareness and skills'.

Spotlight 13: Showcasing ICT

At East London High, several teachers were apprehensive about using technology in their lessons. Some found it daunting. Following a sustained period of staff development, that still did not produce wholesale use of technology among teachers, the school decided to address the issue of 'embedding' technology among teachers through 'showcasing technology'. Teachers were to ensure classroom walls displayed material that supported learning and/or behaviour expectations in their area. They also had to prominently display a 'welcome greeting' in a minimum of three languages spoken by students at the school, among other things.

> We recognized that staff were somewhat apprehensive to use ICT. We supported them by providing professional development opportunities for them. However, we also realized these were never going to lift some teachers out of the state they were in. That is, in order to take them forward, to take our students forward, we had to do other things to get teachers to demonstrate their use of the technology and to develop confidence. As a result, the senior leadership team decided to (a) model ICT at every opportunity we had to do so but especially during assemblies and staff meetings; (b) encourage ICT use among teachers through them regularly updating/changing displays around school and in their classrooms; (c) allowing each subject area to

showcase their provisions via the televisions that are fitted in the reception and canteen areas.

Principal 2, England, female

By adopting these strategies, it was clear that the principal and leadership team were hoping to achieve multiple outcomes:

- focus on the vision and goals of the school;
- show leadership in ICT and provide support to colleagues;
- emphasize the link between technology integration and student learning;
- enhance students' learning and motivation by showcasing their work;
- build confidence and a learning community among staff.

According to Principal Kerry,* these opportunities would deliver the message to staff and students that technology integration is a goal that can be achieved in the school. Teachers being actively engaged with the technology through wall displays, media displays and through teaching was important in terms of whole-school capacity-building for East London High. There are few better or more effective ways of getting people to understand and do something than actually showing them how to do it and/or getting them involved in doing so.

Reflection

The role of the principal continues to evolve, and technology leadership is a recent and ongoing addition (Anderson & Dexter, 2005). Technological leadership is a key ingredient in the effective use and implementation of ICT that results from and is demonstrated by efforts to change and prepare schools and students for the increased demands of globalization and the modern information age (Chang, 2012). In other words, 'the shifting borderland narratives' (Miller, 2012, p. 1) have made it much more urgent for principals to pursue opportunities to deepen the qualitative learning experiences of students in and through ICT. With continued enhancement of digital technology, technological leadership is vital to moving schools forward. A principal's role as technology leader is undeniably important in trying to provide students with an education that is reflective of the times in which they live, and to better prepare them for the possibilities and likely challenges of the future.

Tan (2010) and Grady (2011a), drawing on the work of the Technology Standards for School Administrators Collaborative (2010), provide a useful summary of the responsibilities principals fulfil in their role as technology leaders:

- establishes the vision and goals for technology in the school;
- carries the technology banner in the school;
- models use of technology;
- supports technology use in a school;
- engages in professional development activities that focus on technology and integration of technology in student learning activities;
- provides professional development opportunities for teachers and staff that facilitate integration of technology into student learning;
- secures resources to support technology use and integration in the school;
- advocates for technology use that supports student learning;
- links national technology standards and policies to what is done at school;
- communicates the uses and importance of technology in enhancing student learning experiences to the school's stakeholders.

The discerning and forward-thinking principal who understands the significance of ICT at school and the associated possibilities for individual learners and society will bear these in mind. An effective principal must maintain constant oversight of changes in the ICT environment and also in the needs base of his/her school, since there can be no room for mismatch. For their own effectiveness and efficiency, principals therefore need to be trained in the language and use of ICT, and in particular how to select and apply technology tools to teaching and learning. In addition, they need to provide professional development opportunities to staff that focus on common and new technologies. To counter embedded cultural narratives of deficit at school, principals also need to be constant and consistent in modelling the use of technology, and where possible and/or necessary invite others to do so as well. This is an important part of what leadership is about and is taking leadership beyond mere symbolizing. Principals should also focus on the 'big picture' although in doing so should not put off achieving 'baby steps' which may be harder to achieve in the short to medium term, depending on availability of resources and context, since students will still want to learn to use and engage with technology and teachers and staff will still want to improve teaching and/or other processes, in the meantime.

5

Policy Leadership

There is nothing more infuriating for professionals in the field than the feeling that the latest set of ministerial priorities will soon be superceded by a new set.

Former UK Schools Minister, David Miliband, 2003

Education policy is high on the agenda of governments across the world. Global pressures focus increasing attention on the outcomes of education policy and on their implications for economic prosperity and social citizenship. The experience of each individual learner is therefore decisively shaped by the wider policy environment. However, there is often an underdeveloped understanding of how education policy is formed, what drives it and how it impacts on schools and colleges.

Bell & Stevenson, 2006, p. i

Introduction

Within the last three to four decades, there has been increased interest in educational leadership around the world. The result of this increased interest in leadership has been the proliferation of theories and studies aimed at explaining leadership, its impacts and its effects. Research in both developing and developed countries is contributing to an increasing understanding of how schools and other educational institutions are led and managed (Bell & Stevenson, 2006). Nevertheless, it is worth noting that the practice of school leadership does not occur in a vacuum or on its own and is exercised in some kind of policy context, influenced and shaped by social, historical, economic and cultural issues. As a result, it is important that studies in school leadership reflect this wider policy environment. As Grace (1995, p. 5) points out:

> [I]t is essential to place the study and analysis of school leadership in its socio-historical context and in the context of the moral and political economy of

schooling. We need to have studies of school leadership which are historically located and which are brought into a relationship with wider political, cultural, economic and ideological movements in society.

Grace highlights that a reductionist approach to the study of educational leadership is inadequate (and perhaps inaccurate) since instead of focusing on contextual issues and factors, it places emphasis on quasi-scientific management solutions developed with little regard for contextual specificity. In other words, the tendency to separate policies from the realities of those who must implement and 'live' those policies. Furthermore, as suggested by Hatcher (2005), there is also a tendency to detach studies of leadership from studies of power – in this case national political bases. It is however important to recognize that the practice of school leadership is influenced and shaped decisively by its wider environment, and by the power relations existing within that environment (Bell & Stevenson, 2006). The nature of that environment will be formed by, and from, a range of factors, working against each other or together, unique to each context, in a way that influences and impacts each educational institution within that context. Factors may be social, economic and/or technological and may be applicable to the national and/or international context, or both. Nevertheless, what is beyond question is that, within the field of education, all over the world, and regardless of educational level or phase, the policy context plays a significant part in shaping an institution's internal environment.

The global education sector is in an ongoing process of change and schools and other educational institutions are arguably at the heart of many of these changes. Notions of effectiveness, competition, performativity, total quality management and accountability are prominent components of recent and prevailing discourse in global policy rhetoric about schools. How can schools become (more) effective? How can schools become (more) accountable? How can schools increase their (own) performance, thereby increasing national standing in international league tables? How can schools increase outcomes for students, raising national prospects for growth and development? These are but few of the questions that hover in recent and ongoing debates on school leadership and educational policy. And these are but a few of the questions that principals grapple with on an almost daily basis.

Schools operate in two broad policy environments, the internal and the external, both of which can be as volatile as they are unpredictable. The external policy environment of a school consists of two discrete but interrelated contexts: the supra-national and the national. The supra-national policy context is concerned with international laws and policies that apply to children in all countries. An example of this is the 1989 UNCRC that stipulates that all children, everywhere, have a right to an education provided by the state. The national policy context is concerned with laws, policies and other relevant frameworks that apply only to events and actors within a country. The Child Care & Protection Act (2004) in Jamaica and the Children Act (2004) in the United Kingdom are examples of this. National policies can also be aspirational, for example, in the UK *Every Child Matters* (Chief Secretary to the Treasury, 2003) and in Jamaica *Every Child Can Learn, Every Child Must Learn* (Task Force on Educational Reform, 2005). The external policy contexts relevant to schools in many countries, including Jamaica and the United Kingdom, include central and local government policies as well as shifts in public attitudes and the socioeconomic status of members of the communities that each school serves (Busher & Barker, 2003; Riley et al., 2000). Within a country's internal and external environments there are multiple actors. Internal actors could include the school board, parents, staff and students. External actors could include government, media, suppliers, technology developers and special interest groups such as environmentalists.

The internal environment of a school organization is important to its own effectiveness, productivity and accountability. In other words, the rules and policies produced and agreed upon by internal stakeholders can go a long way in guiding a school towards fulfilling its 'natural' potential and towards achieving the goals and demands set by the actors in the external policy environment. As set out earlier however, a school's ability to succeed will be as much dependent on its own internal abilities, capabilities and strategies as it is related to factors in the national and global policy environments.

In other words, what goes on in schools, what objectives they pursue and their ability to pursue them, what subjects teachers teach and what students learn are, by and large, influenced by national policies and to an extent by the government in power. That is, in general, schools are under obligation to implement national policies at the school level and also to teach the curriculum that has been prescribed by the government, unless they have been permitted to do otherwise. How teachers teach however, and the precise methodologies and approaches used, is usually influenced by internal actors. Chiefly, the principal mediates government policy and the contextualized needs and status of his or her school, thereby, to a large extent, influencing what goes on inside (Miller & Hutton, 2014).

National policies at school level

It is important to note that policies must be viewed as both products and processes (Taylor et al., 1997), and that conflicts and concerns over values and demands are played out as much, indeed more so, in the processes of policy development as in the actual text of the policy itself. In other words, by nature, neither policy development nor policy implementation are straightforward. Bowe et al. (1992) argue that within the traditional pluralist framework, the artificial separation of development from implementation, and the privileging of policy development over policy implementation, results in an over-simplified model of the policy process that fails to reflect the complexity and 'messiness' of policy development and implementation. Indeed Jennings' (1977) linear approach to policy-making has been criticized for being remote and detached from actual implementation. Bowe et al. (1992) however argue that a policy is a product and a process and continues to be shaped and re-shaped, even at the point of implementation. Among principals in this case study, this argument does not apply since they described feeling 'left out' of the policy-making process, although being 'told to implement' policies. I will return to this matter later.

Principals are key players in the implementation of national policies. In a sense, they can be described as gatekeepers to the actions and activities that occur at the school site. Nevertheless, for national policies to succeed at school level, input is required not only from the principal but also from other members of a school community. Ball et al. (2011, p. 626) identify several members of a school community, described as actors, who are directly involved in the implementation of national policies at the school level. They argue that these actors are positioned differently in relation to a particular policy and its implementation, based on their role in a school and based on the nature of their engagement with a particular policy. For example:

- narrators: interpret, select and enforce – usually principals and the leadership team;
- entrepreneurs: advocacy, creativity and integration;
- outsiders: entrepreneurship, partnership and monitoring;
- transactors: accounting, reporting, monitoring;
- enthusiasts: investment, creativity, satisfaction and career;
- translators: production of texts, artefacts and events;
- critics, union representatives: monitoring of management, maintaining counter-discourses;

- receivers: mainly junior teachers and teaching assistants – coping, defending and dependency.

School principals in this study were well aware of the crucial role they play in translating and transmitting government policy to staff, and other members of a school community.

> It is very important to get input from staff about how we can implement certain government policies at school level. There is a limit to how much such input will achieve however, but it is very important for us as a school that staff feel they have been given a chance to consider and debate some of what we are asked to do. There is absolutely no point pushing ahead with a particular policy or a policy in a format [way] that will create or exacerbate tensions rather than result in solutions. This could affect staff morale and adversely affect pupils.
>
> Principal 5, England, male

Principals recognized the importance of hearing discordant voices, among staff, concerning national-level policies, so their implementation could take place in an atmosphere of openness and trust. They noted however that some staff did criticize simply 'for the sake of criticizing'.

> We have some members of staff who are members of a large teaching union. They never see the good in anything. They criticize and criticize and criticize. Sometimes they make some salient points, but other times – I find they criticize out of grandstanding. I don't believe the unions sometimes get that we are all on the same side.
>
> Principal 2, England, female

> We'll never usually get everyone onside, but it's important to talk to staff and to get them to air their views. There may be little that we can change, but if they feel they have been given a chance to air their views, then implementation, even if they don't like what is being demanded of them, is more likely to be a collective endeavour.
>
> Principal 8, Jamaica, female

Opposition to policy implementation is not new. And with the prevailing culture of performativity and accountability high on the agenda of national governments, opposition seems set to continue for some time yet. Regarding labour unions, Ball et al. (2011) suggest, 'Managing and relating to unions is therefore critical …' and that 'carriers of a collective history are sometimes irritants to policy, making "official" interpretations that much more difficult to sustain or somewhat less credible' (p. 632). Thomas and Davies (2005) describe the practice of criticizing simply for the sake of criticizing as a micro-practice of resistance. An assessment of micro-political processes and practices provides that school and other educational institutions are arenas of contestation of values, which guide the implementation of practices, through political negotiations and policy processes (Grace, 1995) and offer an holistic explanation for the interactions of people in organizations (Ball, 2012) and not merely a top-down view, as is common in managerial discourses. Rather, in these interactions participants (senior staff, teachers, support staff, students, parents) are 'actors with their own interests and values that they want to see implemented in practice through the accession of adequate resources to them' (Busher, 2006, p. 31).

Principals know that such resistance should neither be overlooked nor ignored. Furthermore, consensual policy implementation signals collective ownership that can lead to better results. Nevertheless, as Olssen et al. (2004) posit, 'There was a time when educational policy as policy was taken for granted . . . Clearly that is no longer the case. Today, educational policies are the focus of considerable controversy and public contestation . . . Educational policy-making has become highly politicised' (pp. 2–3). Olssen et al's observations are apt, pointing to more activism and interest among the different actors involved in education.

National policy overload

Ball et al. (2011) argue that a prominent feature of current education policy in many countries is the extent to which policy must be seen to be done, is reported done and accounted for. This is arguably the case in both developed and developing countries where policy rhetoric and demands are sometimes separated from the lived realities of schools and other educational institutions, or have become obscured due to the short-lived, sporadic, conflictful and otherwise overlapping nature of some educational policies (Bell & Stevenson, 2006; Miliband, 2003). A constant and fast changing policy environment has implications for overall school effectiveness and for the quality of leadership provided by principals. In England:

> With the changing landscape of government policy, sometimes it's difficult to keep up. It's really hard to make sense of what the government is asking schools and teachers to do. Sometimes it's a bit overwhelming.
>
> Principal 6, England, male

> Changes in the educational policy landscape are making it harder for schools to make sense of their reality. I dare say, even their identities. Today we are a normal

school; next week we are an academy, resulting in all kinds of changes to our funding structure, staffing structure, governance structure and even our curricula offering.

Principal 1, England, male

And in Jamaica:

Reforms to education provide opportunities and challenges for the way schools operate. There are plenty [of] opportunities to get rid of outmoded and outdated practices. But the government has got to be careful to allow principals and teachers to stand still, 'to catch their breath'; to internalize a policy before another one is introduced. Otherwise, schools will be caught in a whirlwind and that could undermine their effectiveness.

Principal 10, Jamaica, female

A common thread among principals is the need for closer coordination and correlation between government policies and the 'on the ground realities' (Ball et al., 2011, p. 629) of principals and schools. Principals suggest they want to be able to catch their breath and 'think through and internalize the spirit and objectives of one policy before being confronted by another, or several others'. Principals also acknowledge that educational policy-making and implementation should link national policies with instructional leadership and vice versa, in ways that foster and promote the academic and personal development of students as well as staff, despite competing interests. The 'policy whirlwind' described by principals is consistent with former UK Schools Minister David Miliband's message to principals that '. . . nothing [is] more infuriating for professionals in the field than the feeling that the latest set of ministerial priorities will soon be superceded by a new set' (Miliband, 2003).

Spotlight 14: Policy overload

A number of principals expressed concern at the number of policy initiatives they were being asked to implement or to consider implementing simultaneously. They understood the need for change and the reasons for change within the education system but suggested there was a mismatch between what government expected and what schools could reasonably be expected to achieve, due to a number of reasons, but due mainly to the unavailability of 'slack' in schools' human resource capacities.

> Multiple reforms are taking place in Jamaica's educational system at the moment. There is much emphasis on accountability through school inspections, on improving the quality of teaching and learning and on the professionalization of teachers. These changes are happening simultaneously, at a time when we have more students in classrooms and fewer teachers being recruited. It seems to me, outputs and inputs do not match and this is making it difficult for schools to deliver on some critical areas.
>
> Principal 8, Jamaica, female

Whereas principals generally understood and accepted the need for, and welcomed, changes to the education sector, there was a sense of exasperation among them of 'being unable to cope' due to a 'policy implementation rush', 'on top of everything else'.

Implementation: practical or idealistic

Principals in this case study reflected on practical issues and constraints that negated their ability and that of their schools to implement a policy in full. They did not always implement government policy to the 'letter of the law', choosing instead to focus on what their school was capable of doing, what would work in their school and how, and whether they had the human and material capacity and resources to deliver in ways that were practical and reasonable:

> The policy guides everything we do. For example, *Every Child Matters* is our overarching framework and we do not veer from that. As a principal, it is my job to ensure that government policies are implemented at school, in what I believe to be in the best interest of pupils. It is my duty to ensure every child gets the best out of their time at school.
>
> Principal 1, England, male

Wholesale, evangelistic implementation that seemingly 'towed the line' was countered with other views of what was practical and realistic, given the different contextual issues facing a school:

> We are very much guided by national policies, but we localize national policies to fit our context. We are committed to the 'Every child must learn' agenda but wholesale policy implementation cannot work at my school. We are a small school with 74 students and five teachers, including myself, located in a deep rural community. Parents of our students are mainly farmers or they are unemployed. As a school, we barely have enough money to cover day to day expenses let alone 'extras'. Whereas policy requirements may be the same for my

school and the one located in an urban area, implementation will be very different – as is the case with my school.

Principal 4, Jamaica, female

This practical view of local-level policy implementation is supported by Riley (2000) who described principals as '... rule breakers ... willing to change in response to new circumstances' (p. 47). Riley's view of principals highlights the notion of risk-taking, a crucial trait among successful leaders. In this case study, principals did not consider themselves as breaking the rules but, rather, bending or reinterpreting the rules:

> The education regulation requires that students wear 'appropriate uniform' to school. Over time this has come to mean: a pair of brown or black shoes, khaki shirt and khaki trousers for boys and the relevant tunic for girls. My school is located in a very poor inner-city community. I cannot punish students for not wearing the 'appropriate uniform' when I know full well their parents can barely find money to feed them. I tell the parents, 'send the children to school . . . just get them here . . . we will teach them . . .'

Principal 10, Jamaica, female

There are several practical issues and reasons associated with any decision not to implement national policies in full, and these are usually weighed carefully and balanced in the context of the work environment. Although all principals want to comply with national policy requirements, their filtering out and selective implementation underlines a common-sense approach to policy implementation that is both contextual and tactical. In other words, it is contextual because the particular characteristics of the environment influence and to some extent determine what is possible, but what is actually implemented is mediated in terms of a knowledge of local issues underpinned by the overarching aim of an institution, in this case schools, and not a particular policy. According to Ball et al. (2011), selective policy implementation by schools is an important aspect of policy interpretation. Furthermore, as proposed by Giddens (1984), people have to assert their agency against both the rules (structures) and the systems.

Spotlight 15: Filtered policy implementation

Principals suggest they are compliant with the dictates of the education department or ministry, but only to a point. In their view, national policies provide an overarching framework of goals. Despite some principals being 'nearly evangelistic' in their commitment to the ideals of national policies, they all agreed that national policies do not make exclusions for context and as a result it was not always practical or possible to commit to the wholesale application of national policies at the school level.

> My school is located in a socially neglected inner-city community in London. Poor achievement outcomes have been a defining feature of this school for years, underpinned by a high rate of staff turnover. However, as a school, we recently took the decision to focus on raising attainment in all subjects at all grade levels and for this year, this is everybody's mission. The government wants schools to focus on 'healthy eating', but as a school, we feel we cannot jump on that bandwagon at this time because we have much more at stake. Don't get me wrong, healthy eating is important, but we simply do not have the staff and resources to focus on implementing a healthy eating programme now. That is something we will have to do another time, perhaps next year. For now though, our focus is on raising attainment throughout the entire school.
>
> Principal 2, England, female

Principals described risking the 'wrath' of the local authority or 'missing out on achieving some government targets'. But they were committed to doing so if this meant they could provide students the best experience possible, consistent with the contextual factors relevant to their school and the community in which the school is located. Principals did not flout the dictates of the education department and/or ministry to prove they were 'above the law' or to 'be at odds' with the authorities. Nor did they risk their jobs or being sanctioned to 'show a policy was flawed'. Rather, they did so in response to external pressures, underpinned by knowledge of local factors in the context of what they believed to be appropriate for their school at that time.

Involving schools in national policy-making

Policy implementation at the school level exacerbates the messy and unpredictable nature of school leadership. International, national, institutional and classroom policies and priorities mix and filter, clash and overlap, and principals are responsible for their effective implementation. Schools, like any other organizations, by their nature are unavoidably complex and messy and their engagement with policy is a constant negotiation, often in a fast-paced and changing sociopolitical context (Rodgers, 2013). But for schools to make sense of national policies and to claim greater ownership of their implementation and successes, principals suggest greater involvement in the policy development process and not only at the implementation stage.

I think governments need firstly to equip schools with the infrastructure and staffing they need; then they can expect all kinds of outcomes. Also, they need to get schools involved early on in the policy process. It's unrealistic to ask schools to 'provide learning that cuts across horizons and frontiers' when we do not even have electricity in classrooms let alone computers. What comes first: the chicken or the egg?

Principal 4, Jamaica, female

Implicit in this reflection is Fullan's position concerning the importance of pressure and support for schools. 'Successful change projects always include elements of both pressure and support. Pressure without support leads to resistance and alienation; support without pressure leads to drift or waste of resources' (Fullan, 1991, p. 91).

Government policy is too 'top down'. More consultation is required with people on the ground. Survey principals and staff and let them help establish the priorities for the next 5–10 years. But to expect compliance simply because 'you are the government and you pay our salaries' is not good enough. Give us a hand in helping to determine the priorities in education so when the policies land our desks, we may just be better prepared.

Principal 8, Jamaica, female

Principals want to comply with national policy requirements in a way that produces deep and meaningful change for students and their families. However, their ability to effect such changes is tested due to what a policy sometimes demands of schools, and also in terms of the manner in which policies are developed and implemented. Principals wanted to feel more in control of a school's direction, although as Lewis and Murphy (2008, pp. 135–6) propose: '... the reality is that, in some respects, many headteachers are more like branch managers [than chief executive officers]. They are handed down expectations, targets, new initiatives and resources – all of which may or may not be manageable in their context'. Lewis and Murphy's observation is quite apt and once more points to a linear approach to policy development and implementation (Jennings, 1977). Returning to Bowe et al. (1992) at this point, they asserted that as policy is 'made' it is constantly being shaped and re-shaped and, instead of being seen as a process, it should be seen as a cycle, made up of 'policy contexts'. This notion is inconsistent with the experience of principals who felt policies were linear and de-contextualized and did not include the voices of, or reflect the realities of, those whose realities (on the ground) the policies were designed to impact. Bowe et al. however highlight a much larger problem. In whose interests are policies made? There is no automatic consensus about policy implementation and development and some principals, particularly those leading schools in rural and remote communities, describe policies as geared mostly towards serving the interests of those schools closest to the centre and to those who are therefore more likely to influence policy debates and decision-making.

School-level policy-making and implementation

As in the case of national-level policy implementation, at the school level principals also play an important role in the successful development and implementation of policies. School-level policies are intended to ensure good order in a school's day to day operational activities. Grace (1995) describes them as affiliated cultures that are constructed, negotiated and projected by a school's leadership team. Busher & Barker (2003) argue that school-level policies are implemented by school leaders to serve as contexts for middle leaders and their colleagues in academic and pastoral departments. This, according to West et al. (2000) implies that school leadership takes place at multiple levels and that school-level policy-making involves distributed leadership (Gronn, 2003; Harris & Spillane, 2008).

> We take a hands-on view [of] the policy development at school. That is, we get everyone involved. It is important to hear multiple voices and have multiple input so whole-school ownership can be assumed from the start.
>
> Principal 5, England, male

> Our middle leaders are important to our policy development and implementation strategy. Not only are we preparing them for senior leadership roles but their involvement is about their own capacity-building in their current roles.
>
> Principal 1, England, male

The role of middle leaders offers insights into how principals are able to get buy-in from staff for school-level policies. As Busher (2006, p. 32) articulates:

> It is these middle leaders, especially in larger schools, who help to create subject related and pastoral policies, often in negotiation with their colleagues, to implement the policies of themselves, of senior management and those required by central government, through the construction of particular practices in the classroom.

Ribbins (1999) argues that all decision-making in schools involves political acts that encompass value-laden choices involving moral, financial, and personal judgments about different courses of action (p. 34). Furthermore, successful school cultures are collegial (Hargreaves, 1994) rather than merely professionally collaborative (McGregor, 2000), underlining the fact that schools operate much more effectively in an atmosphere of equality and respect.

> Our prefect body is also crucial to our school-level policy development and implementation. We actively solicit their views not least because [the] majority of the policies are targeted towards them and their needs, but because we are genuinely interested in how they feel we can make [the] school better.
>
> Principal 9, England, female

The construction of a schools' ethos, although led by the principal, is dependent on all actors in the school, be they teachers, support staff or governors, although it is to be recognized that some individuals have more power than others. Muijs and Harris' (2003) notion of teacher leaders is important at this juncture. That is, there are teachers whose major workload is based in the classroom but who seek to work with their colleagues, outside the classroom, to shape school policy. More to the point, and perhaps more reflective of what happens in the majority of schools, Frost and Durrant (2003) restrict the notion of teacher leadership to people holding non-promoted posts in schools but who take a lead in decision-making beyond the doors of their classrooms.

Spotlight 16: West London High – school-level policy-making/implementation

West London High is led by Edith* who is in her mid-forties. This is her second appointment as a principal and she has been in post for one year. She has a master's degree in education with a specialism in leadership and management. West London High has 110 staff, including 94 teachers, several of whom also hold a master's qualification. There are two deputy headteachers and four assistant headteachers, and just over 1,000 students on roll, taught in year groups between 7 and 13. The school's catchment is mixed and students are from a range of different communities, socioeconomic backgrounds, ethnicities and abilities. Staff are also drawn from diverse socioeconomic, ethnic/race and educational backgrounds. There are 16 administrative and support staff, a small number of whom work with students directly as 'teaching assistants'. The school's canteen is run by an outside agency and security personnel are contracted.

West London High is a relatively new school with modern facilities. It is located in a reasonably 'well off' area of West London, although students from several neighbouring communities within the borough also attend. Over 50 per cent of students at West London High are from middle class families, many of whom are business owners. West London High is described by Edith as a 'modern comprehensive co-educational' institution where 'all are welcome'.

Traditionally, West London High was not as 'open' and as 'welcoming' and the school was plagued by different problems with several different groups within the school calling 'foul'. For example, the school lost its 'outstanding' status which was downgraded by Ofsted only six months before Edith joined. In addition, students were turning up to school late and this had been compounded by 'a somewhat higher than normal rate of absenteeism' among both staff and students. Further, the school had also developed a reputation locally for being 'detached' from the community in which it was physically located and many residents did not really 'identify' with the school or know 'what was happening over there'.

When Edith took over, she immediately set out on a path to make West London High 'truly open and welcoming' by revising outmoded and outdated policies and by introducing new and more appropriate ones. Edith described several challenges she faced in getting governors, staff, parents and even students to 'buy in' to the changes she wanted to introduce. Undaunted, she was 'determined' to make the school a better environment for learning and teaching and that was not only located in a community but was also part of that community. Within the first 12 months of taking up her post, Edith revised the following policies:

- **Anti-racism:** clarifying that the school was multi-racial and racism, under any condition, was not acceptable from anyone in the school.
- **Inclusion:** clarifying that the school values every member equally regardless of race, disability, gender, social class or other perceived difference and that these differences should be actively celebrated.

Also, within the first 12 months of her appointment, Edith also introduced the following new policies:

- **Community cohesion/relations:** clarifying that the school needed to project a positive and wholesome image within the local community and that the school would pursue opportunities to engage with local people, businesses and non-governmental organizations (NGOs). A community cohesion liaison was also appointed.
- **Attendance and punctuality:** clarifying attendance and punctuality for effective performance and reinforcing existing policies for attendance for

teachers and students, respectively. Penalties for any breach were also outlined.

- **Homework:** clarifying that homework was a natural part of schooling which had to be completed regularly in order for students to cover the curriculum areas and to deepen their own learning. Penalties for any non-completion of homework were also outlined.
- **Anti-bullying:** clarifying that bullying of any kind (e.g. playground, staff room) would not be tolerated by staff or students under any circumstances. Penalties for any breach were also outlined.

Edith feels she has done a good job in having these policies implemented. She recognizes that it takes courage to lead effectively but that she also has to set the tone for the school she wants to lead. She concedes that there is still work to do in 'some areas' as some policies are 'working better' than others. She also concedes that there is a slight risk of an implementation gap. However, she suggests that in the 'near future' she and her senior team will look again at ways to more closely monitor the effectiveness/impact of all school policies since 'being accountable' and 'holding each other accountable' are important aspects of her leadership.

Accountability through school inspections

Accountability in education and school accountability have featured prominently in recent and ongoing educational policy discourse. Governments are accountable to their citizens to provide quality education that is 'fit for purpose', delivered through a network of infrastructural inputs in the form of technical, human and financial resources. All this against the backdrop of a wave of school improvement rhetoric and increased competition in the global market for education, increased efficiency over the use of scarce resources and total quality management. In the mid-1980s school improvement was defined as 'a systematic, sustained effort aimed at change in learning conditions and other related conditions in one or more schools with the ultimate aim of accomplishing education goals more effectively' (van Velzen et al., 1985, p. 34). However, since the early to mid-2000s and beyond, school improvement may, arguably, be defined as inspections, inspections, inspections.

In as much as governments are accountable to society as a whole for the kind and quality of education provided by schools to students, principals are accountable to the government, students, parents and the school board, since they – principals – are the custodians of the nation's education system, aims, objectives and outcomes. Put differently, in terms of school accountability, principals are a kind of intermediary, acting on behalf of the state, in the interest of the state, on behalf of students and in the interest of students, and so on. As Balarin et al. (2008) put it, the lines of answerability are not simple or straightforward; rather they are very complicated.

Market forces continue to exert powerful accountability pressure on schools. And no two schools are the same. Further, as Reynolds et al. (2006) point out, each school's history and context will vary. There will be some factors, for example, whether external or internal, that are simply beyond a school's control. In addition, some factors may be of a longer-term nature, for example, poverty and the social mix of students at a school. Other factors may be more medium to short term, for example, staff turnover and student mobility. At the same time however, if student achievement outcomes in a school decline or do not improve in the manner expected by those acting on behalf of the state and other stakeholders, parents will be less inclined to send their children there. This could lead to important consequences for the school, as a result of such decline or lack of progress. For example, a school could find itself with reduced resources resulting in the quality of provision for existing students being less, coupled with the demands of those who may join. At the same time, teachers may not be as motivated to work or to work as hard in that environment, leading to further staff loss or unproductivity among staff (MacGilchrist, 2003).

Carnoy et al. (2003) distinguish between internal and external accountability in schools. Internal accountability derives from a sense of responsibility among individuals in a school, and external accountability is concerned with constraints and demands placed on schools represented by performance measures which schools are expected to meet and improve upon and through meeting the requirements of an external agency or body, such as an inspectorate. Principals work at the boundary between internal and external forms of accountability, prompting Coulson (1986, pp. 85–6) to highlight that in addition to being 'goal orientated; personally secure; sensitive to the dynamics of power inside and outside their schools; analytic; in charge of the job' (p. 85), principals are also 'tolerant of ambiguity' (p. 86). As internal accountability issues have already been discussed in Chapter 2, the remainder of this chapter presents principals' reflections on their perceptions of and/or interaction with external accountability systems.

Principals viewed school inspections as a particular kind of challenge directed towards testing their own leadership and efficacy, as well as the overall effectiveness of schools. Nearly all were preoccupied with the inspectorate (Ofsted in England and the NEI in Jamaica), whether or not their school had been inspected. Some were concerned about the validity of the inspectors' judgments and how these had or could impact a school's, and their own, reputation; others were critical of the inspection process, suggesting it provided only a 'point in time' indicator of a school's effectiveness and performance. Some believed the inspectorate was not sensitive to contextual factors in a school's local and/or internal environments.

> My school has not been through the inspection system as yet, and I am not looking forward to it. I read the reports and I hear the stories in the media and leadership and management are always to blame. I know the buck stops with the principals but sometimes there are other factors at play that prevent a principal from doing a better job. But those other factors will not get reported in an inspection.
>
> Principal 8, Jamaica, female

In line with these reflections, Linn and Haug (2002, p. 35) suggest that:

> [T]his volatility results in some schools being recognised as outstanding and other schools identified as in need of improvement simply as the result of random fluctuations. It also means that strategies of looking to schools that show large gains for clues of what other schools should do to improve student achievement will have little chance of identifying those practices that are most effective.

A number of principals suggested that school inspections were also a public audit of their stewardship, and felt uneasy about by this type of personal and professional assessment.

> Inspections are stressful for the staff and for myself as a principal. I have been through two and they have been a mixed bag. Where we thought we were strong the inspectors disagreed and as a result we received an unsatisfactory grade. That did put a massive strain on us to improve and lots of staff became demotivated and hard to reach. It was a bad time for me as a leader because I didn't think we were that bad, and getting staff motivated after the inspection had passed, and prepared for another one, was a nightmare. The entire experience was a nightmare. But second time round, they judged us as satisfactory.
>
> Principal 7, England, male

Mortimore and Whitty (1997) have argued that 'setting unrealistic goals and adopting a strategy of "shame and blame" will only lead to cynicism and lowering morale amongst those teachers at the heart of the struggle to raise the achievement of disadvantaged pupils' (p. 10). Similarly, Southworth (1995) proposed that when a school undergoes an inspection, principals felt it was not so much that there is a lot at stake but rather it is they who are at stake!

> School inspections make me very uncomfortable; very vulnerable; very exposed. There are so many things that can go wrong. Inspections are definitely tests of a heads' leadership. Don't get me wrong – I want my leadership to be assessed; after all, the taxpayers are paying my salary. But I just wish there was a different way to assess my stewardship and the performance of my school.
>
> Principal 2, England, female

It is debatable that inputs from the public purse require public accountability measures defined and kept afloat by 'naming and shaming'. As Fullan (2001) notes, there is a 'need to place education at the heart of a wider approach to social and economic renewal' (p. 235). Further, 'It is exceedingly difficult to combine accountability, incentives and capacity building as evidenced by the fact that no government has ever done it effectively' (p. 232). Even though many principals were somewhat fearful of the consequences they may face (e.g. job loss) and the repercussions for a school (e.g. exodus of staff and students) as a result of a 'failed' inspection or a 'low grade' from an inspection, they still felt it was important for their stewardship of their school to be assessed against similar schools within an education zone, borough or even a country. This they felt was a 'fairer' way of holding them to account.

Spotlight 17: Jamaica Primary – internal accountability

Jamaica Primary is led by Erica* who is in her mid- to late forties. This is her first appointment as a principal and she has been in post for one year. She has a master's in educational leadership & management. Prior to her appointment she was vice-principal and she has been at the school for 15 years. Jamaica Primary has 45 teachers, including Erica. Many of her staff also have a master's qualification. There are about 550 students on roll who are taught in in year groups from 1 to 6. The school has two dedicated staff who clean the classrooms and maintain the furniture and property. There is also a 'chef' and other ancillary staff who work in the 'tuck shop'. The school secretary doubles as Erica's administrative assistant. The school has modern flush toilets located outside the main building for students and two toilets for staff located inside the staff room.

Jamaica Primary is located in a rural part of the country on a parcel of land overlooking the sea. It is in close proximity to hotels and resorts in an area known for 'eco-tourism'. Local businesses support the school by helping to finance refurbishment and also by paying for trophies and medals to recognize students and teachers at certain events. The area surrounding the school is quite calm. The school is fitted with electricity, Internet connectivity and a functional computer lab with 25 computers. There is also a specialist ICT teacher.

In 2012 Jamaica Primary was inspected by the NEI which graded the school as 'failing'. It was the first time Jamaica Primary had been inspected, in what was the first wave of island-wide inspections by the newly established inspectorate. The outcome of the inspection, which was made public, dampened the morale of students, parents and teachers, ultimately leading to the resignation of Erica's predecessor. As a result, Erica was asked by the school board to act as principal, and very soon afterwards she was confirmed as the school's next principal.

Erica had a clear vision of what she wanted for the school. She wanted Jamaica Primary to be the 'best school in the parish'. She called meetings of parents, teachers and students. She met with officials in the regional office of the education ministry and she also met with the school board, setting out her vision and how she thought it could be realized and what support she needed.

Erica introduced weekly lesson plan checks for teachers to be overseen by the vice-principal. She also introduced a period of common planning on Wednesday afternoons for two hours after the students leave for home. These are compulsory. In addition she introduced a period of six-weekly lesson observations for all staff, led by herself and the vice-principal. Lesson observations had a clear assessment rubric and each would focus on a different issue each time, for example, behaviour management, lesson transition, teachers' mastery of content and assessment objectives and strategies.

Parents were also encouraged to 'get students to school on time' and to 'improve attendance'. Furthermore, parents were encouraged to work with students on completing their 'out of school activity packs' which contained extension tasks and homework. These were given out at the beginning of each six-week period.

Twelve months after the 2012 inspection, the inspectorate returned to Jamaica Primary. They saw decisive and visionary leadership at work. Underpinned by improvements in learning and teaching, and by a more 'focused' staff and student body, Jamaica Primary received an improved grade of 'satisfactory'. Although happy about the progress the school has made, Erica realizes there is much more to be done, but she also realizes that when internal accountability measures are in place and where they are robust, it makes it easier for schools to meet external accountability requirements. Erica and her team continue to implement changes aimed at making the school an 'excellent' place – for all.

Reflection

Schools do not operate independent of the state as the state sets the parameters and conditions for how they can operate in the education sector and in society. The state has certain outcomes it wants schools to achieve and also has certain preferred ways it wants schools to operate. In an environment where there are hundreds and thousands of schools it makes sense that the government plays a central role in the 'what' and the 'how' of schooling. Nevertheless, there are several tensions between what a government expects and what is practical or even reasonable for a government to expect, based on the peculiar characteristics of schools. Unfortunately, government policies usually do not make space for peculiar characteristics of individual schools and as a result principals feel they must bend the rules, challenge the dictates of government and, where required, justify their actions later. But such outcomes can be avoided where principals are invited to contribute to the policy development process.

Policy development and implementation at the school level is however quite different. Although there is the central element of politicking that goes on where principals enlist the support of key teachers to seek and obtain widespread buy-in, in the main, school-level policy-making and implementation are often seen as more consensual and inclusive. In other words, they draws their meaning and influence from the different actors who contribute to the shaping, reshaping and delivery of such policies.

The whirlwind of policies in education impacting the ability of principals to do their jobs effectively is problematic. Similarly, a whirlwind of school-level policies can rob schools of (already) limited time for teaching and learning activities. Schools cannot function without policies, nor can an education system. Nevertheless, dialogue between different parts of an education system can potentially lead to more effective engagement and therefore better results, for all, in the long term.

6

People Leadership

Key factors in any debate about leadership are: the importance of leader self-development; the need to act to ensure learning is kept at the centre of everything school leaders do (learning-centred leadership); and the notion of leading the development of others. It's not what leaders do themselves it's what they do with and for others that matters. Leaders need to be able to reflect critically on and challenge current practice.

Earley, 2013, p. 3

In most cases, little monitoring or control of teachers and teaching is required and leaders create favourable conditions to enable teachers to do their work independently. This includes leaders protecting teachers from disturbing external influences, overseeing administrative tasks (buffering), whilst facilitating opportunities for professional development, staff alignment, feedback and resource provision.

Scheerens, 2012, p. 146

Introduction

People leadership is important business. People leadership focuses attention on 'the human side of enterprise' (McGregor, 1996), by attempting to align and meet the different needs of members to those of an organization (Maslow, 1950). As McGregor states, 'There is no one size fits all theory or practice; there are no Ten Commandments for motivating people' (p. 9). And in a school environment, where there are multiple personalities and competing interests, people leadership is serious *political* business. Effective people leadership requires a principal to show commitment to organizational learning, understanding and empathy towards diversity and ambiguity, and to be forward thinking and creative in relation to how best to meet the needs of members at all levels of a school. All these however require a significant investment of time from a principal. Time to provide direct guidance to an individual; time to attend to paperwork; time to explore, pursue and present opportunities; time to reflect and review; and time to invest in new and additional inputs as appropriate. The availability of and the need for (more) time has however been regarded as a problem for principals (Brighouse, 2007).

In many large organizations, especially those run by leaders with only limited or no experience and/or training in people leadership, there is a greater likelihood that the goals and objectives being pursued will be missed or muddled. This is equally applicable to schools. Peters (2013) proposed that effective people leaders:

- care for everyone in their organization and have a genuine interest in them;
- celebrate the achievements of people and not just the achievements of the organization;
- correct mistakes in a supportive and responsible way by suggesting alternative approaches;
- compensate people in the organization by being willing to fight for all and not just for some.

Peters' views reflect a key principle in transformational leadership of showing 'individualized consideration' to members of a (school) community. Additionally, these views align with Senge's (1990, 2006) view of learning organizations where everyone has opportunities to grow and develop as an organization also grows and develops. For Senge, leaders – for example, school principals – need to have an overarching view of what learning means both in and for a school organization. In a school, learning *in* the organization has almost always received greater focus, although in recent years, and due to the deepening performativity culture, there has been more attention on learning *for* the organization. In a sense, the pendulum has swung, and a byproduct of performativity is learning in schools that focuses on all who study and work in them.

Schools will approach people leadership and organizational learning issues in a way that reflects their individual context and capacity. As mentioned earlier by McGregor (1966), there is no 'one size fits all'. As a result, different suggestions have been made in terms of approaches that involve the whole-school environment (Leithwood & Jantzi, 2008); that focus on student engagement (Leithwood et al., 2004); and that involve collective learning across formal organizational roles and boundaries, since these have been shown to have a strong positive influence on classroom practice (Spillane, 2006).

Developing staff

Developing staff can take many forms although the expected outcome is usually the same – that is, to make them better at what they do, for the benefit of an organization and its clients. The central role played by principals in developing their staff is well documented. Nias (1980) found that teachers respect a principal who they thought showed interest in their professional development. Principals in this case study also reflected on the importance of supporting and promoting staff development:

> We consider staff development a priority. We can't demand that staff do X and Y and ... not support their professional growth and development. We consider our school to be a learning organization, and we have to demonstrate that we are serious about building up everyone.
>
> Principal 8, Jamaica, female

> We are located in an inner-city area and as a result we have a higher than usual turnover of teachers. To retain staff, we have bought into all kinds of fast track schemes, supported by a range of professional development opportunities. From time to time we also 'buy in' bespoke programmes for [the] whole school on issues such as child protection. By trying these different approaches to teacher development, we are hoping this will go some way [to] increasing their commitment to us and in building their capacity to do their jobs [more] effectively.
>
> Principal 2, England, female

Some specific professional development approaches are discussed in the following two sections, grouped as 'internal' and 'external', based on how they are arranged and delivered to staff.

Internal professional development

Principals reflected on ways they support teacher development through internally arranged and delivered approaches and opportunities.

Mentoring

Principals generally recognized the importance of mentoring and, where possible, assigned school mentors to staff, especially early career teachers. Some principals also took on the task of directly mentoring others.

Despite my 60-hour week I still find time to mentor two colleagues. I would like to be able to mentor others but I have very limited time to do so. But I think it's important for those aspiring to become school leaders to see how challenging and demanding school leadership is and for them to know what they will have to commit to when they become leaders.

Principal 6, England, male

Mentoring for certain groups of teachers was also seen as very important:

It is a legal requirement that newly qualified teachers (NQTs) are assigned a school mentor, usually that teacher's subject leader or head of department. We recognize however that subject leaders and year heads (grade coordinators) are the operational 'hub of the school' and so they are well placed to bring other teachers up to speed in a short time. Further, we consider the heads of departments and year heads part of the school's 'extended leadership team' and through our once-monthly meeting they too receive critical insights into school leadership by meeting with the senior leadership team.

Principal 5, England, male

Being a mentor carries significant responsibilities if the mentoring activity is to be beneficial to the individual being mentored. All principals recognized this with one going a step further to admit, 'At times I feel I could do with a mentor … just someone who could be a safe space for me to speak openly' (Principal 3, Jamaica, female).

Spotlight 18: Suburban High Academy England – people leadership

Suburban High Academy England is led by Tom* who is in his mid-forties. This is his second appointment as a principal and he has been in post for five years. He has a master's degree in education and is also undertaking doctoral studies in education. Suburban High Academy England has approximately 250 staff: 200 teachers including Tom, three deputy headteachers and five assistant headteachers. There are approximately 2,000 students on roll who are taught in year groups from 7 to 13. The school recently converted to an 'academy' and the principal now therefore has greater autonomy over the school's curriculum, staffing and pay decisions. With the school's new academy status, the principal is now referred to as the 'chief executive'.

The school has a range of modern amenities and facilities to support teaching and learning. It is located in an affluent town, close to a quay and two universities.

Many students who successfully complete sixth form usually get 'good' to 'excellent' results and go on to university. The school is one of three secondary high schools located in that part of town. Students are from homes where mostly two parents work, although in a few cases only one parent works; in even fewer cases (less than 100) students come from homes where no parent works.

Tom has a broad view about staff development that is inclusive and orientated towards the whole school. For example, at any one time, at least five or six teachers will be studying for a master's qualification that the school pay towards. In addition, there are in-house programmes on different topics such as 'action research' for teachers and 'coaching and mentoring' that are delivered to teachers with specific areas of responsibility. At the end of each school term, there is an evening, complete with snacks and drinks, dedicated to colleagues sharing their research, etc., through poster- and/or paper-based presentations. The school also publishes a half-yearly educational research journal that shares best practice and highlights research undertaken by staff.

In addition to these approaches, the school is involved in different kinds of partnership working that has seen administrative and support staff spending time outside school on 'mini-secondments' and groups of staff and students travelling to other countries to participate in various learning and development activities that simultaneously add an international dimension to the school's curriculum and also build whole-school capacity.

The school also runs an extensive CPD programme in-house for teachers on various topics including: 'behaviour management', 'assessment strategies' and 'child protection & safeguarding', some of which are also open to other categories of staff and school governors (board members).

Shadowing

Shadowing is an effective approach to introducing junior staff to the demands and some of the 'behind the scenes workings' and experiences of a job role to which they aspire. Shadowing was not as well developed and utilized a practice among principals compared with mentoring, although it was still viewed by them being an effective approach to staff development.

> Shadowing provides insights to the teacher doing the shadowing that other professional developmental approaches are unable to provide. I didn't get that chance before I became a principal but I think it is important for prospective principals to have this invaluable opportunity.
>
> Principal 6, England, male

We offer an opportunity to 'shadow' to any teacher who wants this opportunity. But we can only do three teachers per year [one each term]. Shadowing [is] 'deep' and riveting and opens up the eyes of the person doing the shadowing to so much more than you can tell them. Obviously, there are some cases and matters that are excluded from the shadowing process due to confidentiality issues, but the shadowing experience itself is the closest experience *to the real thing*. Even though shadowing is time consuming, I think it should be encouraged and used more widely in promotion and progression rounds so more teachers could benefit.

Principal 9, England, female

These examples position shadowing as an approach to staff development that is invaluable, deliberate and purposeful. In other words, principals believed shadowing was able to provide teachers with new insights into teaching, leadership and other issues they would not usually be exposed to with such detail, and the insights gained were useful in scaffolding a teacher, possibly for their next move up the career/promotions ladder.

Unpaid 'promoted' work experience

Providing teachers with unpaid 'promoted' opportunities was another approach used by principals to develop staff. While not ignoring the potential moral dilemma associated with the decision to assign teachers to a job role that carried no scope for long-term promotion or short-term remuneration, principals also focused on the necessity of having job roles filled and the practicalities involved in running a school.

There are many jobs that need doing in order for the school to function at its best. And we are only in a position to pay for those that have been 'established'. So, we would say to teachers, 'Do this job for a year. It will be good for your professional development, your CV. And you can use the experience for the next job you apply for whether in or outside this school.' So, our position is twofold: get the job done and give that teacher a chance to build capacity and enhance their skills.

Principal 2, England, female

Other practical issues associated with assigning teachers to these unpaid roles were also discussed:

The school could not function without teachers taking on unpaid roles. We can only hope that they will garner good experience and skills through these assignments that can benefit ... their career progression. Teachers sometimes resist doing these jobs, but in the end they come round to the understanding that we are all working towards the same goal – the success of our students.

Principal 8, Jamaica, female

Teachers make an enormous contribution in time and effort to the success of students. In doing so, they make untold sacrifices, in return for which, where possible, principals provide them with opportunities to hone and harness their skills in leadership or in a particular specialist area.

External professional development

Principals reflected on the ways they support teacher development through externally arranged and delivered approaches and opportunities.

Exchanges and visits

Some principals supported and were themselves involved in international collaborative partnerships that resulted in cross-border visits. These were positioned as positively contributing to the international dimension of a school.

We recently hosted a group of teachers and principals from Jamaica at our school. This was brilliant for both our pupils and staff – from a very white part of the UK – to see so many Jamaicans in our school in one go. We learnt so much about their culture and educational system. Since the visit, the senior leadership team and governors agreed that we should establish a partnership with at least one school in Jamaica. This is important since our school clientele is changing to reflect pupils from more diverse backgrounds.

Principal 6, England, male

We've taken staff and pupils to three or four countries in the Caribbean, Africa and South-East Asia. We've also hosted teachers and principals from overseas at our school. As a school, this has been critical for us in helping students to build their profiles as global citizens and for staff to develop useful linkages. For staff, teaching from the UK-produced textbook is not always enough or even the best. From these visits, our staff have picked up useful tips and have also clarified curricular content issues in subject areas such as history and geography – climate change and recycling – for example.

Principal 2, England, female

And as a result of these visits and collaborations . . .

We are considering the appointment of an international development partner to help us manage and sustain our partnership projects. We are keen to capture and document the impact of our collaborative efforts on staff and students. A key focus of our partner will be to help us document impact case studies, drawing on feedback from staff and students and also from our partners in the countries we've visited. We intend for the impact case studies to contribute to the sustainability of our partnerships and also provide the Department for Education, and some of our critics, with examples of teacher-pupil exchanges that actually work.

Principal 1, England, male

One principal reflected on her own participation in an international study tour:

I visited England in 2013 as part of a study tour and capacity-building exercise. I learnt a lot. My view of what it is to be a school leader has completely changed. I have been a principal for eight years, but my observations of practice and interactions [with] school leaders in England left me feeling that I can do more, I must want more, for my students and staff. The study tour has been one of the single most important events in my entire professional life because it has given me an exposure and a worldview I didn't previously have and it has simultaneously shown me how much more I need to learn and do to be a more effective principal.

Principal 10, Jamaica, female

The benefits that can accrue to staff and students based on their direct or indirect participation in an international study visit cannot be measured in dollars or pounds. And this added value should not be ignored. Mitchell and Sackney (2000) describe individual, interpersonal and organizational benefits that can accrue from participating in carefully organized and appropriately planned study visits and tours. As discussed in Chapter 3, for international partnerships to work they require serious investment in time, effort and energy. Nevertheless, as principals continue to interpret and reinterpret their own and their school's ability to provide learners with a qualitatively different educational experience, directed towards their personal, social, emotional, economic and spiritual development, a child's best interest remains the central focus of a principal's decision-making, thereby justifying all reasonable actions taken towards this end.

Support for university courses

English principals confirmed that, where possible, schools provided financial support for teachers who were studying. Some schools would pay up to 50 per cent of course fees up front but this was in cases where the subject of study or the topic for the final dissertation or project was directly linked to an area of interest for the school.

> We have 20 teachers currently studying. All are investigating a topic or an area linked to our school improvement plan. Sixteen are taking their master's and four are doing doctorates in education. As a school, we pay 50 per cent of all fees, up front – directly to the institutions. This is our commitment to our staff. We are investing heavily in them.
>
> Principal 7, England, male

Not all English schools are able to supplement the course costs for teachers who are taking advanced university qualifications regardless of the perceived or actual benefits that could accrue to the school. However, where a teacher needed time off to study or otherwise prepare for an exam, this would normally be facilitated:

> Unfortunately we do not have the budget to pay tuition costs for teachers. But where we can, we allow them time off to prepare for their examinations.
>
> Principal 5, England, male

Jamaican schools do not provide up front monetary support for teachers who wish to pursue advance qualifications. Rather:

> Teachers and principals who are studying will have to pay up front. However, the ministry [of education] usually reimburses half the costs after successful completion – where the topic or subject was education related and teachers usually receive an additional increment in pay on successful completion of their studies. Furthermore, teachers can get up to two years study leave with pay, based on years of service ...
>
> Principal 3, Jamaica, female

Regardless of how costs were to be met, whether by an education ministry or department, a school or a teacher, staff development was recognized to be a key factor in a school achieving medium- to long-term objectives and contributing to its overall success.

Secondment

Principals were in agreement that a 'secondment' activity can be a useful professional development opportunity for an individual and also a school.

> I think allowing staff to take on secondment activities is very important. There is so much for them to learn and take back to us. Indeed, there is also so much of what we do here that they can share. But I think it is a useful thing for them to

have another experience in another environment, especially at a somewhat higher level, where they can impact in a wider way.

Principal 5, England, male

Although, in the main, principals supported secondment opportunities for staff, there was still some tension among them as some argued that secondment opportunities appeared to entice teachers to want to leave their teaching job, whereas others argued such opportunities provided teachers with excellent skills and knowledge from which schools can and do benefit on their return.

All teachers, especially those with 10 years' service or more and who have not been promoted, should get the chance to experience a secondment activity. This I feel would give them a chance to share and to develop. It would make them less frustrated and give them an opportunity to do something different and to learn something new . . .

Principal 6, England, male

There are only few opportunities for teachers to progress in the system. Secondment provides an opportunity; an escape even. Whereas we would love for teachers who go on secondment to return to us and share their skills and new knowledge with us, to make us better, we understand if they do not want to come back to teaching at the level of the classroom.

Principal 2, England, female

The dilemma presented by the principals in this study is perhaps the same or similar to those faced by other principals in education systems globally. There are only limited opportunities for teachers to develop and even fewer for them to progress in their careers. And where opportunities to develop and progress exists elsewhere, for which teachers are suitably qualified, principals have to balance the right of a teacher to develop and the requirement of providing students with suitably qualified and experienced staff, even if that sometimes means making unpopular or even political decisions about teacher development (Hirsh, 2010).

Spotlight 19: Principals as CPD gatekeepers

The tensions highlighted in this section are indicative of wider tensions in the sociopolitical, economic and cultural environments of a school.

I have allowed one of my teachers to go on secondment to the ministry of education. This has been extremely useful for us as a school as we have benefited from her contacts, her new knowledge and her experiences. From time to time she would come in and lead professional development seminars for us on particular issues she's learnt. This has gone a far way in improving our teachers and their understanding of these issues. So, having her on the 'inside' has been good for us as a school.

Principal 8, Jamaica, female

As principals try to 'connect the dots', they usually do so in a way that ultimately advantages their school. But decisions about what works, what works in this school, what works at a particular point in time and what works for an individual are all heavily mediated by the principal's own view and vision of what an individual teacher wants and how the principal feels about it. They are also heavily mediated by where the school is in its trajectory and whether the principal feels the school can *afford* to release (or support) the teacher at this time or if at all.

Staff recruitment

As discussed in Chapter 2, the availability of suitably qualified staff is a key ingredient in a school's quest to achieving excellence for students. Teachers can drive or retard students' progress through their enthusiasm (or lack of), their experience (or lack of), their commitment (or lack of) and their skills and qualifications (or lack of).

Staffing a school can be a huge challenge for principals. Sometimes you are 'this close' to recruiting somebody who looks really good on paper. You make an offer and they turn you down or the references that come back are not what you expected.

Principal 5, England, male

We've have had temporary staff in school for up to two terms because we strongly believe we should invest the time necessary into finding the 'right' person. The [school] board also supports this view. We've had up to three separate recruitment rounds in order to find a suitable subject leader for mathematics but still no luck. And the worse part is, we are not that impressed with the temporary staff [member] who is covering.

Principal 2, England, female

Other staffing decisions are much more challenging:

A few years ago we had a vacancy for one teacher but ended up recruiting two. On the day of the interview we were really impressed by both teachers. That did mean for a time we were somewhat overstaffed, but we were able to use the skills of the one who was under-timetabled in other areas of the school such as in learning support and pastoral care.

> Principal 9, England, female

There are times when you have to make temporary quick fix appointments and hope that someone proves themselves because, on paper they don't look that good and in the interview they were not that impressive. But, when your hands are tied and you have students to be taught, you have to get someone in, even in a temporary post.

> Principal 6, England, male

Sometimes we have to offer prospective teachers much more than we normally would do especially in a subject area that is hard to staff. We've had to do this to teachers of mathematics and physics.

> Principal 7, England, male

Having the right team of staff, especially teachers, in place is one of the most important decisions for principals. Increasingly, in both developing and developed countries, and in line with ongoing challenges in the global economic environment, education is being positioned as the 'panacea' to the problems of societies measured in terms of economic growth and development. I will return to this economic-motor metaphor in Chapter 8. Suffice to say at this point however, school staffing issues in terms of numbers, gender balance, qualifications and subject specialisms, level and type of experience, are some of the less than straightforward issues principals have to regularly resolve in trying to provide students with an education that caters to their total development needs.

Staff disciplinary – letting someone go

Staff disciplinary matters usually involve some degree of stress for principals. Taking everything into account, they usually consider a range of alternatives before reaching a decision to sanction a teacher.

Letting a teacher go who refused to carry out lesson planning:

> We've had to let someone go recently. After several warnings and much support, he still refused to plan and evaluate lessons. Students were complaining that they weren't learning enough and four observations of his lessons confirmed this. He received support from the assistant head with responsibility for CPD but he continued to go to class without lesson plans and therefore had no way of showing

what he had covered or how well pupils were progressing. We simply had to let him go. He was a lovely chap, but he didn't possess good teaching habits.

Principal 1, England, male

Terminating employment through a redundancy exercise:

We've had to use compulsory redundancy to weed out between 10 to 12 weaker teachers. Two rounds of voluntary redundancy had not been successful in getting them to jump before being pushed. The labour unions didn't like the compulsory redundancies and they threatened to disrupt school. But, I was clear: 'you cannot work here if you are unable to cut the mustard'. I received support for my decision/approach from the governors and the local authority, although I faced criticism even from colleagues on the senior leadership team. Today our school is in a much better and stronger position ...

Principal 7, England, male

And for poor practice:

We have a newly qualified teacher (NQT) at school who did not pass her mandatory one-year probation this year. She doesn't have a clue. She doesn't know how to plan lessons, set learning objectives, give students feedback and manage behaviour. We've extended her probation by one term and we have given her clear targets to meet each week for the next six weeks. However, if after eight weeks she is not cutting the mustard, we will [instigate] 'capability proceedings' against her. We'll be left with no choice but to let her go. I think it's a heinous crime she was allowed to pass her PGCE and awarded a teaching qualification. I am beginning to seriously doubt whether she is cut out to be a teacher.

Principal 9, England, female

The reflections above once more confirm that school leadership is not black and white. Principals are tasked with leading the development of the human talent and education ministries and departments, and parents trust them to do so, and to do so effectively invariably involves difficult decision-making.

Working with the school board

As we've come to realize, schools are very important institutions. And in order for them to perform to expected nationally accepted (or other agreed) standards, it is essential they are not only well led but also well governed (Balarin et al., 2008). School boards or school governors, may be thought of as a group of 'agents' or 'middle men' (*sic*) with important internal and external accountability functions. They are responsible for keeping the principal accountable to students, teachers and parents and they are also responsible for ensuring that the benchmarks and standards set by the government are being applied and met. As a result, it is perhaps not difficult to see why the relationship between some principals and their school board might be fraught.

> The board chairman and I do not always see eye to eye, and over time this has created tensions in how the board is able to function. This has sometimes led to slower decision-making as well as resulting in the least feasible decisions being made. As a principal, it's hard to run a school with my hands tied behind my back by the board.
>
> Principal 5, England, male

And slightly more worrying:

> My board chairman is a prominent member of one of the two leading political parties in the country. Sometimes he opposes reasonable suggestions made or decisions taken by myself and supported by other board members. It is a shame when the education of our children is treated like a political football and when good decisions taken are blocked for politically motivated reasons.
>
> Principal 4, Jamaica, female

Other principals reflected on more positive experiences:

> The board is very supportive of my leadership and we enjoy a relatively good relationship. We disagree from time to time and we disagree strongly sometimes, but our disagreements have never prevented us from coming back together to carefully scrutinize and consider the decisions we've taken or need to take in order to improve our school.
>
> Principal 3, Jamaica, female

The tensions presented by principals are perhaps reflective of tensions in other schools and education systems worldwide. A satisfactory working rhythm between a principal and a board of governors can only emerge over time based on understanding, respect and trust. However, Dean et al. (2007) found that school boards that played largely a supporting role compared with a strategic role were not as effective in helping to shape the strategic direction of a school.

Working with the education ministry/department

Like a school board, principals also work very closely with the education ministry or department, whether they are a part of a system that is centralized or not.

These relationships are crucial for delivering a good educational experience to students. Working closely and harmoniously with the education ministry or department is crucial, if not practical, to the successful implementation and delivery of national policies – as discussed in Chapter 5.

> I would describe my relationship with the regional office as a challenging one. We just do not seem to be able to agree on the 'best' approach to move the school forward. This really does set us back because a school needs the support of the ministry and the ministry needs the support of principals. But it's not always easy to support policies and programmes led by persons who are not in the field and therefore do not know our realities ...
>
> Principal 10, Jamaica, female

Another also proposed:

> I would say it is essential for a principal to have a functional relationship with the local authority. They are your first port of call, really. But definitely you would not want to have conflicts. They are the ones you will turn to for support if something goes wrong. And something can go wrong – even for a headteacher.
>
> Principal 6, England, male

Tensions in the relationship between a principal and an education department or ministry are not new. Such tensions can definitely lead to 'hardships for a principal', according to one principal. Education ministries want principals to thrive and principals want schools to do well. Miller & Hutton (2014) encourage principals to work harmoniously with their education departments despite the prevailing policy environment and/or personal qualities for the good of students and the greater good of society.

Working with parents

Principals shared contrasting experiences of working relationships with parents. That is, in any one school, it was always possible to meet a range of different parents who provided a tapestry of experiences and challenges.

> Parents are important to what we do. We can't succeed without getting them on-side. But there are some 'pushy parents' that simply stress me out. I mean, 'they want you to work miracles with their child'. It's always about what the school hasn't done; what the teacher hasn't done, but never about what she is doing at home that can distract the child or what she hasn't done to build upon what we are doing at school. Honestly ...
>
> Principal 6, England, male

> Some parents think they are experts on education; on teaching and learning. But that says a lot about how much they think they know about education since they bring their kids to us to teach. We received over 50 complaints last year for things like, 'teacher didn't ask my son a question'; 'I don't think he is getting enough homework'; 'he wasn't given a leading role in the end of year production'.
>
> Principal 4, Jamaica, female

Tensions between school and home, teachers and parents, are not new. Webb and Vulliamy (1996) reported that principals were having to protect their staff from parents by intercepting and fielding criticisms themselves.

> Staff are sometimes harassed by threatening notes, telephone calls and emails from parents who are annoyed about something. It is important for myself or another member of the leadership team to intervene at this point. But, not all parents are hard to work with; some are really kind and supportive.
>
> Principal 5, England, male

An important part of the principal's job is to provide reassurance and support to teachers (Acker, 1990). Jones (1987), however, argues that 'Protecting staff from anxiety is not, in the long term, a helpful headteacher skill', and that 'complacency' can develop, thus limiting further innovation for school improvements (p. 153). Jones' view does not match those of principals in this case study who argued it was their 'duty' and 'responsibility' to protect staff so they could 'focus on teaching and learning'.

Dealing with school bereavement

The death of an individual can leave those left behind with a range of, sometimes, conflicting emotions. Although not all principals in this study had experienced a school bereavement during their time as a school leader, all spoke of the 'crippling' impact the death of a member of a school can have on the entire school community.

> We used to have a teacher here, Mr H. He died a few years back. He was involved in a car accident. He died on the spot. He was at school that day and was heading home. It wasn't even his fault. His death still haunts me. He was such a lovely person. His loss was a massive shock to everyone. He was a good teacher and he was popular and well respected by everyone.
>
> Principal, 6, England, male

I have not had the experience of a member of school passing away. And I really don't want to have that experience. I have seen my colleagues going through that and it is extremely stressful. I have seen them go into 'overdrive', doing all kinds of things to help out the family. In a sense that helps them to deal with their personal grief – but I don't want to have to face that. I don't know how I would cope.

Principal 8, Jamaica, female

There is no formula for dealing with bereavement (Sherrington, 2012). Principals were noticeably uneasy when talking about this issue, with some expressing 'deep' concern for their own emotional well-being and that of staff and students. Whereas they fully realized that they had no control over 'matters of life and death', they also admitted to being 'upset, at even the thought' of losing a member of the school community.

Spotlight 20: School bereavement

Dealing with bereavement is never easy. Schools tend to see themselves as a community, although less attention is given to the fact that a community is comprised of different 'family' and other relationships. Each form group and each teaching group in a school could therefore be considered a separate family unit, which is part of a larger school community. So when a member of staff or a student dies, this can result in a severe impact on the emotional health and well-being of a school as well as on teaching and learning.

Last year we lost a little girl aged 10. She'd been diagnosed with leukaemia nearly a year earlier and she'd been receiving treatment for it. She was a class prefect: well behaved, reliable, polite. Her sudden passing shocked the entire school community and there is no one at school who didn't 'feel it', especially her classmates and class teacher. Her death was two weeks before the end-of-year examinations.

Principal, 3, Jamaica, female

Bereavement not only tests the principal's leadership and social awareness, it simultaneously examines a school's ethos and its 'soul' – challenging, questioning, valuing, shaping, re-shaping, positioning and re-positioning. In other words, there are no textbook scenarios that can be suitably applied. However, how the death of a member of a school is managed can, simultaneously or at one point in time or another, lead to feelings of isolation, support, frustration, reflection and hope, all of which could contribute to the continued effective functioning of that school community.

Isolated working

School leadership can be a fulfilling and cathartic experience, but it can also be a long, arduous and lonely one. Principals spend an enormous amount of time 'behind the scenes' lobbying for their schools, attending meetings and events, responding to the demands of the education ministry or department and completing paperwork, for example. As a result, some have come to experience social and professional isolation, due to decisions taken or not taken, through being detained by hours of paperwork, and from urgent and sporadic activities, issues and meetings requiring attention or resolution.

> Sometimes I can't sleep properly at nights because I am anxious about a decision I took today or one I am about to take; or simply due to events at school. Sometimes I agonize over decisions long before and long after they are taken, just to make sure that within myself I feel confident that I will or that I have made the best possible decision about someone's life or career or about a particular purchase. This vulnerable, stressed, lacking in confidence side of being [in] school leadership is not one seen by the staff and parents, my deputy or even the school governors.
>
> Principal 10, Jamaica, female

An annual event that arguably fills many principals with mixed emotions leaves at least one feeling very stressed and anxious:

> When examination results are in, in mid- to late-August, this is usually an anxious although exciting time for the entire school community. There are usually lots of insightful and very reflective questions from staff about the strategies and resources they used the previous school year to support students and whether these were appropriate or adequate. Results day itself is pretty perplexing and each time, no matter how often I experience this, I pray for the day to come and go without incident: without tricky questions from the governors, without being confronted by angry parents and without the scrutiny of the press if things did not go as well as we'd have liked. You just never know what to expect . . .
>
> Principal 9, England, female

Whereas principals in this case study described the joy and pride of whole-school success, many described the personal cost and pain that accrues to their personal and family life due to their job role and work demands:

> I went to work on Good Friday this year. I got in at 9.15 a.m. and I didn't leave there until 9.24 p.m. There was so much to do, so much to quietly focus on. But

being able to work like this has an obvious cost to my personal life and also my family life . . .

Principal 6, England, male

As far back as 1994, Pollard et al. found that many principals face isolation in carrying out their role. When considered against a principal's personal and family life, the reality that school leadership practice is not black and white is once more brought to bear. Ironic is the fact that as principals devote their energies to producing best outcomes for their schools, extended hours at work can lead to physical isolation and break up of their own families. Further and better research on how the families of principals are impacted due to their job roles and demands is needed to guide policy and practice in this area.

Spotlight 21: Performativity and family life

All principals agreed that although they enjoyed their jobs and the satisfaction that comes from being able to contribute to individual-level and social change, they also found their jobs to be 'highly demanding', 'stressful', 'onerous', 'lonely' and at times 'overwhelming'. Principals wanted the best for their students – for them to excel, for them to 'beat' last year's results, but they realize that these aims and objectives come at a high price, sometimes even to them or their families.

> My wife always says to me, 'You are married to your job'. And the truth is, sometimes it does feel that way. What is hard for me is that there never seems to be any let up in demands from the ministry, so no matter how much work you put into a school, there is always [something] else to do or something you could have done differently. I think the people who dream up the policy demands think we are machines and that we are not entitled to a family and social life.
>
> Principal 5, England, male

Principals described 'early mornings' and 'late nights', weekend and holiday working that seem to be compounded by a dynamic policy environment. Many expected late nights and early mornings, but some were wholly unprepared for the job 'taking over my life'. They blame the performativity culture and the policy environment, although soberly proposing: 'you have to do what you have to in order not to slip down the league tables'.

Reflection

There is an apparent paradox of motive towards people development among school principals driven by a raft of equally different but equally compelling purposes. Whereas some principals do what they do to please or out of fear of the ministry or education department, or to secure a school's placement in the league tables, others are driven by the need to improve performance and standards in schools. It is clear that the introduction of standards-based education, high-stakes accountability through testing and inspection, coupled with an invasive culture of performativity, have led to the job of a principal becoming more complex, more critical and more demanding. The ability of principals to understand and respond to the needs of staff and students is an important element of people leadership. This has sometimes resulted in great good and sometimes in anything but. Nevertheless, effective principals respond to the needs of their followers so as to motivate them to greater and better things.

As Hirsh (2010, p. 130) reminds us,

> Career development has to deal with the tensions between the needs of the business and the interest and the aspirations of individual employees. This means talking to everyone about very personal things, such as how they see themselves and what they want from work. Organisations are pretty inept at dealing with their employees as real people – it is a messy, challenging and, therefore, uncomfortable thing to do.

There are a range of people issues in any school, no matter its size and no mater its context. It is easy to *talk* about how to create a school where students can fulfil their aspirations. Without learning for teachers in the context of practice, however, very little can be accomplished. And without practice in the context of learning, even less will be achieved. Put differently, people leadership that involves professional development and support must be at the forefront of a school's strategy for achieving its aims and objectives. Education departments and ministries, along with principals, need to always be mindful of this interlocking relationship.

7

Entrepreneurial and Safety Leadership

Headship is less to do with managing a steady-state school organisation and more to do with anticipating and responding to new initiatives, challenges and opportunities.

Hall & Southworth, 1997, p. 166

Leadership is bound in culture and context and there's no one way of leading. To deal with the challenges in our schools and in society, we need authentic leaders who are humble and self-aware, and who step into the leadership space for a purpose – to make a difference. We also need to weed out those 'mis-leaders' who do harm to the places they claim to be leading.

Riley, 2013, p. 42

Introduction

Recent and ongoing changes in the global environment are making it necessary for schools and those who lead them to 'do education differently' (Miller, 2012, p. 9). Changes in the economic environment, increased competition between schools, increased competition within school and for school places, the publication of inspection results and performance league tables, and a more informed, demanding and discerning consumer base are but few of the factors and issues prompting schools to reinterpret and redesign their approach to education. As a result, schools have become more self-critical, reflective and more inclusive in terms of their outlook and actions, made visible in and through the types of programmes or courses they offer to students, and how these are delivered.

By necessity, what has emerged is a wave of entrepreneurial thinking and acting among schools and principals. Entrepreneurial leadership, according to Roomi and Harrison (2011), means 'having and communicating a vision that engage [*sic*] teams to identify, develop and take advantage of opportunity in order to gain competitive advantage' (p. 3). Implicit in this definition are three important characteristics of successful leaders: foresight, strategy and teamwork. Entrepreneurial leaders need to be in tune with their external environment and to anticipate changes in this environment. Similarly, they need a plan that establishes and clarifies how schools will (continue to) improve. This plan requires creative and 'out of the box' thinking. Furthermore, successful leaders recognize that no leader is an island and therefore enlist the collective capacities of other team members to guide a school's path and to solve problems. Roomi and Harrison also suggest that entrepreneurial leaders lead their organizations through a variety of means, for example, through relationships and culture, in addition to command and control and the ability to handle and deal with the risk, uncertainty and ambiguity in an increasingly risky environment.

Using Roomi and Harrison's definition, and based on the three suggested characteristics of entrepreneurial leadership, I argue that entrepreneurial principals use a 'corporate mindset' to apply skills and behaviours associated with entrepreneurialism to impact their schools. In other words, they are willing to take risks, to innovate, and to make the 'systems' work in a way that benefits rather than constrains what they are trying to achieve for and through their schools. This corporate mindset is about having a 'presence of mind' despite constantly changing conditions in a school's external environment. This presence of mind enables them to find new and different ways of ensuring their schools remain relevant to its mission and to learners. As suggested by Hall and Southworth (1997), 'Headteachers must demonstrate a model of educational entrepreneurialism that seeks to preserve the integrity of the educational enterprise by using rather than being used by government reforms ...' (p. 165).

Spotlight 22: Inner-city Primary Kingston, Jamaica

Inner-city Primary Kingston is led by Trudy* who is in her early fifties. This is her first appointment as a principal and she has been in her current post for eight years. However, she began her teaching career at this school over 27 years ago. She has a master's in educational leadership & management. Inner-city Primary Kingston has approximately 75 staff including 60 teachers including Trudy and one vice-principal (female). A number of her staff also have master's qualifications. There are approximately 800 students on roll who are taught in year groups from 1 to 6. Inner-city Primary Kingston is located in a relatively poor community in West Kingston that is an enclave to political factions belonging to Jamaica's two major political parties. Sporadic violence between opposition factions has resulted in the cancellation of lessons for up to a week at a time.

The school has modern flush toilets, a canteen and a computer laboratory for students with 30 desktop computers. It also recently established a VLE. In 2012, Trudy rallied the local community, staging two major community fayres which netted over JMD$200,000 (about GB£1,300) which she used to purchase and install two large water tanks at the school. This installation means the supply of water at the school is more consistent and there is now a 'back up' should the water board decide to ration supply, for instance, during times of 'drought'.

Many parents in the community do not work and many of those who do operate roadside stalls. There are several stalls located just outside the school's main gate where a small group of food/snack vendors and members of the community congregate. A number of young men can also be seen riding bicycles and/or playing football nearby.

Trudy has an excellent relationship with the members of the community and she is very highly regarded. Community members support school events and projects and trust that Trudy is doing everything possible to provide the best educational experience and outcomes for their children. The school consistently performs well in the national grade 4 and grade 6 examinations.

Sometimes, and depending on the 'intensity of the uprising', when there is a flare-up of violence in the community, Trudy and her staff and students are given a safe passage to and from school. This is not always easy to judge. However, Trudy has established a pact with the community that 'no matter the extent of the violence on the streets or in the community, it should not spill over in the school'. As a result, despite sometimes intense fighting and gunfire in the community, students at Inner-city Primary Kingston can feel 'relatively safe' inside their school, confident that no one from outside will enter the premises and commit a crime or disrupt teaching and learning. Trudy describes her school as 'an oasis in the heat' arguing that '... Parents can always feel reassured that no matter what is going on outside, their children are safe with us at school. This has been a major reason why our teachers generally stay on and ... why we are oversubscribed each year'. The newly set up VLE is expected to play a huge role in times of community uprisings.

Entrepreneurial leadership in practice

Principals in this study showed entrepreneurial thinking in different ways. They explained how they'd used a range of different entrepreneurial behaviours as they tried to gain new students and staff, and retain existing staff and students and other stakeholders, while improving public perception of and confidence in their schools. Principals understand the market conditions for schools, and the role of parental choice in education – especially in England – often describing ways of 'selling' their school, which they felt they could do and did. A number of creative approaches are presented below.

Changing curricula to fit the needs of learners

Principals are well aware that the primary business of a school is to educate and develop students. They are also aware that the student base has changed and continues to do so, and as a result schools are now having to respond to new and different needs. They are also sufficiently clear about the need to provide students with an education that is responsive to and develops their moral, social, intellectual, technological and cultural interests (UNCRC, 1989).

> One of the things we do best as a school is our ICT provision. For years we had only two computer laboratories and no virtual learning facility. A few years ago, as a school we decided this wasn't good enough, so we fundraised for a VLE, which has been up and running for three years now. This is so that on 'snow days' or if a student misses a lesson for whatever reason, he or she can 'catch up' using the VLE. Teachers are always on, assessing quizzes and responding to queries. And teachers tell me that sometimes the questions that do not always get asked in class either because someone is shy or because someone wasn't paying attention get asked on the VLE. But, we know this facility has helped us to reach students in different ways. Parents knows this too.
>
> Principal 5, England, male

> We are the only primary school in the education zone to have two functional computer laboratories. The government helped us furnish one, but the Parent Teacher's Association (PTA) fundraised for and built the second one. One of the local internet companies also provides free internet access all year round. Our students are very poor and many do not have a computer at home. So for us to be able to show them a computer and how to use it and then connect them to the internet is introducing them to a totally different world. But they are the technology generation so they need this exposure. It's important for them.
>
> Principal 3, Jamaica, female

Other principals described the importance of teaching and learning activities being organized in a way that supports the needs of all students, but especially those with physical and/or other disabilities.

> We have four students who are physically disabled. We do not have lifts at school and so we have timetabled lessons on the ground floor. Three of those students

have to use a wheelchair to move about. It's no use telling parents their children can't come here because we do not have this and we do not have that. It's important that as a school we practice what we preach and make our school accessible and inclusive to everyone. It's about inclusion and respect.

Principal 10, Jamaica, female

Despite infrastructural, institutional and economic challenges, some principals were resolute about providing subjects that could be accessed by students of all abilities and interests:

We have students from a range of backgrounds and abilities at school. And as a school, we took a decision about three years ago to revise our curricular offering. We replaced a certain international qualification with A levels and BTECs. Not only have results improved year on year, enrollment has also increased. Parents, students and teachers are now much more confident about their chances of success.

Principal 2, England, female

We constantly review our provision because we want our students to do well. We want our school to do well and to improve in the league tables. We now run 'applied' qualifications alongside the regular GCSE qualifications so that our students are given more choices based on their learning needs.

Principal 1, England, male

Some principals reflected on the issue of gender in relation to the choice of subjects students are offered:

For years we've had a situation where boys' achievement in certain subjects was not as good as that of girls. We've now set up a 'working group' to examine what can be done to address this situation. We want to be able to tell parents, we cater to the interests of both girls and boys in equal measure.

Principal 2, England, female

These issues show that principals are responding to the changing demands and needs of the students in their schools. Whereas this is not always easy, their actions are aimed at improving the life chances of each student and the overall effectiveness of their schools. Hall and Southworth (1997) proposed that 'An issue for school leaders now is whether they interpret their role as managerialist or emancipatory and how they can most effectively contribute to successful schooling' (p. 151). Based on their reflections, principals constructed and interpreted their role as one that extends well beyond 'managerialist', and in so doing they demonstrated critical emancipatory tendencies directed towards the success of individual students and entire school communities.

Spotlight 23: Show and tell

The examples above point to several changes in how education is conceived by schools and how, as a result, a school is positioned in the minds of the consumers (parents) and users (students). Although it is important for principals to note how well their schools are doing and, as a result, shift the narrative away from one of deficit, there was something 'uneasy' in how a schools' provision was being communicated and 'positioned'. That is, a school's success was being objectified and rarified almost as a 'one-off' or a 'coincidental occurrence' rather than being examined in the context of being part of a wider strategy for sustainability. In other words, it was not how well a school was doing that was showcased, rather, it was how well particular sections of a school were doing or how well a school was doing at a particular point in time that was showcased.

> We have one Year 10 male student who is visually impaired. We also have one Year 8 male student who has a hearing impairment. As a result, we have begun providing teachers with additional training in British Sign Language in order to support them. We also impress upon the teachers who teach the student with the hearing impairment to 'face the class when speaking and to speak slowly and clearly so the child can follow'. Our visually impaired student is supported by a teaching assistant in all lessons and all teaching material is printed or photocopied and developed in a font size of 32 so he is better able to see. What we are saying to parents is, 'bring your child here – we will ensure they learn'.
>
> Principal 9, England, female

There was no ambiguity or uncertainty among principals that a school's clientele was constantly changing and they were also clear that methods, processes and systems at school also had to change in order to appropriately respond to changes in their environment.

Resources and material to fit curricula and future needs

Principals reflected on having the appropriate material and resources for learning and being able to provide these in desired quantities. There were two distinct views on this issue, contextualized in terms of two different societies with two very different education and economic systems.

For English principals:

I try to get the appropriate levels of material and resources for students year round. This is essential to their success. We can't ask them to pass examinations without giving them the tools to do so. Some courses require only textbooks, but others require other kinds of inputs in terms of laboratory equipment. It is important that we are seen to be providing the best educational experience for students.

Principal 6, England, male

For Jamaican principals:

We simply do not have money to buy textbooks for students. We operate a book rental scheme but this is not well supported as several parents cannot afford it. This places an additional burden on teachers to develop teaching and resource material. But oftentimes our students are without books and essential material for conducting experiments in science, etc.

Principal 4, Jamaica, female

The differences portrayed above are as powerful as they are symbolic. Teacher creativity is a key ingredient of successful teaching. And so is resilience. And whereas both resilience and creativity cannot simply be plucked from thin air, they can be seen as forms of entrepreneurialism that make teachers and principals want to innovate and provide students with the best possible educational experience and outlook despite social, economic or other variables.

Inclusive practices

Inclusion was a significant area of focus for all schools and nearly all principals were keen to present a good image of what their school was doing to demonstrate inclusion. Two principals commented:

We are an inclusive school with inclusive practices driven by an inclusion policy. Our students and teachers are drawn from different backgrounds and ethnic groups with over 40 languages spoken by students and teachers. We also have students at school who are visually impaired and a few who are physically challenged. Our teachers have experience of planning and leading lessons in diverse classrooms. We are big on equal opportunities in this school.

Principal 5, England, male

> We have [a] system in school where we encourage students to be friends with others. Over the last two years, with help from the prefects, this has now grown into 'friendship circles'. These 'friendship circles' have had a positive influence on all students – those doing the befriending and those being befriended. This scheme has also helped to reduce the number of students being suspended or expelled.
>
> Principal 3, Jamaica, female

The views of the principals reflect, more broadly, schools that are 'emotionally intelligent' (Parker et al., 2006), taking steps to ensure students' emotional needs are met in addition to their cognitive needs. Principals, although expressing reservation about many government initiatives, continued to employ creative strategies in an attempt to meet the learning needs of their students (Brown & Lavia, 2013).

Behaviour management

Placing students at the centre of what schools do in terms of managing behavioural issues was another key entrepreneurial approach used by principals to 'sell' their schools.

> We will not say all our students are well behaved. But what we do have is a robust behaviour management team that is proactive in tackling poor behavior through working closely with parents and carers and other agencies.
>
> Principal 5, England, male

> Our students are really well behaved. We get compliments from people all the time telling us how smart they look in their uniforms and how well behaved they are on the buses and in the taxis. We get stories of some even giving up their seats on buses for the elderly.
>
> Principal 8, Jamaica, female

Keeping parents informed and getting their buy-in in terms of approaches to managing poor student behaviour is crucial to the success of several school-based policy initiatives, and principals were in no doubt as to the value of such relationships.

> We have a very strict behaviour policy that is well supported by parents. Parents know that we want what is best for their children and they trust us to manage the behaviour of the children in the ways set out by the policy.
>
> Principal 9, England, female

Despite strict behavioural policies and robust systems for managing poor student behaviour, a noticeable feature of the perceived effectiveness of this entrepreneurial approach among principals was the opportunities for engagement and partnership with parents.

Quality and experience of staff

As discussed in Chapters 2 and 6, the staff, especially teachers, are vital to the success of a school. Principals reflected on the capacity, skills, experiences and qualifications of teachers and how these are believed to contribute to the success of their schools, thereby including them in their 'sales pitch'.

> A key selling point for our school is the quality of our staff. Our teachers are well qualified and experienced in their field. Some hold advanced qualifications and a number of them mark scripts for different exam boards. We also [have] staff in administrative roles with good experience in industry and in the child protection services.
>
> Principal 1, England, male

> I have a very experienced group of teachers. Year in, year out, they take students through the examinations with very good success. There are other inputs of course that contribute to the performance of our students, however, our students could not achieve in the way they have done without the quality and experience of our teachers.
>
> Principal 2, England, female

It is well known that teacher quality is important to the success of schools and, as previously discussed in Chapter 6, staffing decisions are sometimes not without controversy. Nevertheless, when principals feel available staff are able to 'cut the mustard' they will use their success and/or other special characteristics in the marketing or 'showing off' of their schools.

Examination results

Good examination results are perhaps the easiest measure principals use to sell their schools:

> Examination results are always trending upwards. Parents and carers are interested in how well schools are doing; and we do all we can to ensure the information about our success is accessible. Bad news travels fast, so we must ensure we get the good news out there. This is important for us.
>
> Principal 6, England, male

A school's performance in exit examinations is absolutely crucial to it retaining the continued support and confidence of the community. Our annual results are not yet 50 per cent for all Year 11 students getting a pass in at least five subjects with a grade of at least A*–C. However, in the last four years, our GCSE results have moved from 18 per cent to 48 per cent. This is massive improvement worth celebrating. We put this information on our website and in our newsletter so members of the local community can see how well we are doing.

Principal 5, England, male

An important issue for principals was that parents and a school's local community should know how well a school is doing. This, they felt, was important in gaining their trust and support, which, in their view, had the potential to lead to other 'spin off' benefits, such as partnership working and/or financial contributions.

Safe and orderly environment

Principals were explicit about selling their school as an orderly and safe learning environment. Despite challenges in the immediate school environment, particularly for some Jamaican principals, their ability to 'secure' their school and continue providing teaching and learning under adverse conditions was an important entrepreneurial feature.

We pride ourselves in providing a safe and orderly learning environment for all students. They know the rules concerning uniform, where and when to eat, playing in the corridors, being out of lesson during class time, chewing gum, spitting and fighting. We can boast about how strict we are because in being strict we know we are contributing to a new social order in society.

Principal 3, Jamaica, female

Many principals described schools as active learning spaces where students are not only 'given' information, but also where they are taught to question, challenge and problem-solve.

We do not have the best facilities. We do not have adequate facilities even. But what we have inside school is order and safety. Parents know that their children are safe here. For at least 50 per cent of our 800 students, their attendance at school has become an oasis from the deprivation and thuggishness that is the daily diet in their local communities.

Principal 10, Jamaica, female

Principals were well attuned to the social circumstances of their students and to conditions in the local communities surrounding their schools or in which their schools are located. Schools that had done well in difficult locations and/or under challenging circumstances had 'earned the right to boast', and showcasing success could lead to improved community participation and increased staff motivation.

Spotlight 24: The school as a market and a product

Similar to their evolving role as technology leaders, principals described their entrepreneurial leadership roles. Some were excited at being able to 'boast' about their schools, which gave them an opportunity to increase their networks and to affirm their 'position in the hearts, minds of the local community'. Others were however challenged by their increased entrepreneurial role, describing it as a kind of 'do or die situation' which had resulted from 'increased competition' and 'the fragmenting of the education system'.

Principals therefore interpreted and engaged with entrepreneurial leadership in three different ways. The first set welcomed and embraced being able to 'sell' or market their school and its provision, since 'my school is delivering the goods'. The second set were apathetic and did not engage with the 'selling' or marketing process beyond what the school would *normally* do in any given year. This position came from the fact that these principals believed their schools already had an established reputation and further 'selling' would lead to additional enquiries and applications that were not likely to be successful. The third set tried to evade and/or did not engage with entrepreneurial leadership on the basis that the 'ministry should be doing that' and 'parents will send their kids where they want to, no matter what you do, no matter what you introduce, no matter what you say'. All three approaches provide different insights about principals and how they viewed themselves and/or their school and what a school had to offer. These differing roles require further investigation. Despite the tensions, however, principals were all agreed that schools had become products in their own right and it was their responsibility and duty as school leaders to ensure students and the public/community remained interested in the product, and that there were adequate amounts of prospective buyers for that product, secured through appropriate 'market positioning'.

Enterprising partnerships

Schools enter into partnerships with each other and/or other agencies for a range of reasons. However, decisions to enter into partnerships for strategic and curricula fitness were found to be problematic on the basis that 'I will be judged for my patch' and 'I can't get distracted by a school that is below us on the league table'.

> We are part of an education zone. Not all schools in the zone are as strong although each school has something to offer. It's important that 'stronger' ones partner with weaker ones, helping them to 'come up to the level required'. But, it is also important that stronger schools enter a partnership, believing they too can learn something ... they too can get something.
>
> Principal 1, England, male

> We partner with schools abroad. This is good for our coverage of the curriculum. Our students need to have the best experience possible. Kids in England tend to live in a 'bubble' and our partnership with schools outside the UK is directed towards getting them a 'real life learning experience' of certain curricular topics.
>
> Principal 2, England, female

These views were broadly consistent with North-South partnership research conducted by Edge et al. (2009) which reported that students in the UK benefited from such partnerships in terms of their appreciation and understanding in terms of content and context knowledge.

> We partner with schools that are as strong as or even stronger than us. As a principal, I am being judged on the progress of my school and I have to enter into those partnerships that are most likely to create success for my students and their families.
>
> Principal 5, England, male

> Any partnership we enter into must be to our advantage – whether locally or internationally. The local authority tried to 'force' some partnerships, just over a decade ago, but these failed miserably. I think schools have to enter into partnerships on their own terms and also agreeing the intended outcomes on their own terms.
>
> Principal 6, England, male

A similarly restricted view was echoed in terms of local community business partnerships.

We partner with local businesses so our students can get a 'head start' on what may be required of them in the real world of work, through a period of work experience. This is the only kind of partnership we feel we can take on as a school as the other kinds of partnership engagements would simply distract us and create extra work for everyone.

Principal 4, Jamaica, female

Resolving these tensions is not easy and is beyond the scope of this book. However, the focus of principals on providing students the best learning experience should not be overlooked. Despite differences in beliefs and attitudes towards the value of partnerships and how these should be arranged, all principals wanted success for their students and by extension their schools, consistent with their vision for the school and where they felt the school was *currently* in relation to that vision. Nevertheless, the seemingly inverted view of systems leadership among some principals is worth further examination.

Spotlight 25: Partnership working

Principals wanted to provide a rich educational experience for students. However, it was also clear that some were more committed to and more creative in seeking and pursuing opportunities for their students to engage meaningfully, and to learn from and learn about others outside their schools – including partnerships with local and international bodies. Some principals were driven by the need to provide students a *worldly mindset* (Wenger, 1991), arguing that the curriculum alone could not provide students with the kinds of knowledge and skills needed to function successfully in the twenty-first century.

> Effective school partnerships can lead to benefits for young people, schools, the wider community and employers. They provide opportunities to recognize achievement, increase participation in community life and volunteering, increase awareness of diversity and inclusion, enhance employability, reduce exclusions from school, enhance learning, improve relationships and enhance the voice of young people in community planning and decision-making.
>
> Principal 6, England, male

Not all principals were upbeat or positive about partnership working. In fact, some saw partnership working as time-consuming and leading to distractions from their core business of teaching and learning. Some principals also spoke of staff resistance to partnership working on the basis that this could create 'more work', did not result in 'more pay' and that it also led to a reduction in curriculum time.

There are clearly two very different sets of experiences and perspectives among principals in terms of partnership working. However, what remained constant and well articulated was the fact all principals want their students to have the best educational experience, which some interpreted to mean 'going the extra mile' and 'taking risks', whereas others interpreted this to mean 'delivering the set curriculum' and being creative with that curriculum.

Safety leadership

The health and safety of staff and students is an important duty and responsibility for school principals. Health and safety law in the United Kingdom, for example, places a duty of care on principals and on a school board to ensure systems are in place to protect the members of a school community from harm or injury (see the Health and Safety at Work Act 1974). Although not explicit in Jamaica, the health and safety of all students at school is implied in the Child Care and Protection Act (CCPA, 2004). It is assumed that the duty of care placed on principals to ensure the safety and protection of members of a school community is the same in most countries, even where there may be no formal law or policy in place to enforce this duty.

Health and safety leadership must be guided by essential principles of respect and requires strong and active leadership from principals. In addition, to be successful in developing a culture of safety and respect, principals need to engage with and involve others within the school in this process. Furthermore, there has to be continuous assessment and review, aimed at preventing, identifying and managing risks (Health & Safety Executive, 2013).

Duties of principal and staff

A principal has to take reasonable steps to ensure staff and students are not exposed to anything that risks their health and safety. This applies to activities on or off school premises. In the United Kingdom, for example, the *Management of Health and Safety at Work Regulations* 1999 require employers to:

- assess the risks to staff and others affected by school activities in order to identify the health and safety measures that are necessary and, in certain circumstances, keep a record of the significant findings of that assessment;

- introduce measures to manage those risks (risk management);
- tell their employees about the risks and measures to be taken to manage the risks;
- ensure that adequate training is given to employees on health and safety matters.

In addition to national health and safety guidance or in the absence of the same, principals are encouraged to develop a set of health and safety arrangements in the form of a school policy. The specific policy brief will vary depending on the size of the school and the risks associated with the school's activities. Another consideration may also be its location and type. For example, the policy for a small infant school may be very brief, whereas that for a large secondary school with a range of laboratories and workshops may be more elaborate. As well as the duties and responsibilities of principals, existing United Kingdom law (as noted above) also requires employees to:

- take reasonable care of their own health and safety and that of others who may be affected by what they do at work;
- cooperate with their employers on health and safety matters;
- do their work in accordance with training and instructions;
- inform the employer of any work situation representing a serious and immediate danger, so that remedial action can be taken.

The Department for Education (2013) recommends that staff should follow any health and safety procedures put in place by their principal. The DfE also sets out that teachers and other staff in schools have a common law duty to act *as any prudent parent would* when in charge of pupils. The notion of teachers acting *in loco parentis* is highly accepted in school environments all over the world, whether a formal policy on health and safety exists or not.

Spotlight 26: Physical safety and security issues

Outer London High is led by Tony* who is in his fifties. This is his third appointment as a principal and he has been in his current post for six years. He has a master's qualification. Outer London High has approximately 120 staff with 100 teachers including Tony, two deputy headteachers and six assistant headteachers. There are approximately 1,200 students on roll who are taught in year groups from 7 to 13. Outer London High is located in an affluent area of a north London borough. The school is a recent build with very modern amenities and facilities.

Outer London High has a good mix of ethnicities among its staff and student populations. The majority of students are from middle-class backgrounds, although approximately 10 per cent are from working-class backgrounds. Parents are very active in the life of the school and usually provide generous financial support to the school.

Tony and his senior leadership team have a strong commitment to the physical security of staff and students and also to the security of the 'school plant'. For example, as a new build the school is fitted with modern and up-to-standard equipment and lighting. In addition, there are two separate lunchtime slots for students so as to reduce congestion in the canteen. Similarly, there are designated toilets for Year 7 students only. There is a large car park with clearly marked spaces for staff and sixth formers, bicycle parking and disabled and visitor parking. There are also separate entry and exit gates for vehicles and a separate pedestrian gate.

Against the backdrop of in-school fighting, and some fighting involving students at school and persons in the community, Outer London High introduced an electronic gate complete with entry barrier and a video buzzer system. In other words, all persons coming into school once the morning bell has gone, and before the end of the school day, must be buzzed in and they will be recognized via the video system by the reception staff ahead of being allowed in. The introduction of this electronic gated system has led to a reduction of 'unwanted' visitors coming on site during the school day.

The school has also installed CCTV cameras in the computer labs, in the school car parks, at all entry and exit points to the school building and inside the lifts. The decision to install cameras in the lifts was hotly debated but won approval from the school board on the basis that there were several students with physical disabilities (some of whom require wheelchair access) and if there was an emergency they could be better supported. Furthermore, cameras around the school also contribute to more cooperative and positive behaviour among students. Cameras in the computer labs have resulted in students who steal being caught and to students who access pornographic and other banned websites being found out.

Child protection

Principals recognized the significance of online safety for staff and students as well as the importance of the physical and bodily safety of staff and students, whether based on a school's site or at off-site at events organized by a school. They were cautious that students should not do anything that would cause harm or injury to each other. They were also resolute that staff have a duty of care to students which meant they should protect and seek to protect them to the greatest extent possible. Shielding students from acts of physical and/or sexual violence, especially on a school's site, was a prominent issue for principals.

> We have a zero tolerance approach to offences against students, especially sexual allegations. I lead a primary school and any act of aggression and/or sexual violence against a student is simply unacceptable.
>
> Principal 3, Jamaica, female

> We have a designated child protection officer. We run child protection training for all staff, not just teachers, at the beginning of the school year in September. This is a whole day's training, usually in partnership with the local authority. It is intended to equip staff with skills to detect abuse, usually some form of physical abuse. We have a strict reporting procedure which we encourage all staff to follow, and there are no excuses for not following it. We try very hard to ensure our students are safe.
>
> Principal 5, England, male

A common thread in the views of principals is that of trust. Principals are accountable to students and their families. They have a legal duty to ensure the safety of all students on-site (or off campus on school-related activities). When presented with particular challenges however, their decision-making was less clear cut, forcing them to draw on their experiences in guiding their decisions about how each individual concern and/or case should be handled. The tensions are clear, once more highlighting some of the more difficult decisions principals must take to secure both staff and students. Nevertheless, Sikes and Piper (2010) reported that a number of adults who worked in schools have had their careers cut short or destroyed due to false accusations and allegations made by students.

Spotlight 27: Safeguarding dilemmas

Ensuring learners are safe was an important issue among principals who saw this as non-negotiable. Principals recognized the influence of new and social media on staff and students and that as a result they would have to regularly remind staff to 'be careful not to overstep the mark' and to 'watch out for signs' and also for students to 'not put themselves at risk' and to 'be careful'. New and social media was recognized as posing a particular risk, but it was only a small part of a range of safety and security issues staff and students were faced with on a daily basis.

> We try at all times to act in the best interest of the child. We've however learnt from experience and we've taken the decision as a leadership team that, before referring a case onwards to the local authority or to children's services be investigated, we'll conduct our own in-school investigation first. This is not with all cases, so this is very much on a case by case basis. This is because we do have students who lie about what teachers are alleged to do or have done. This is not to say there aren't some teachers who get involved with students. And those who do should be appropriately sanctioned. However, I have seen the personal and professional lives of colleagues ruined due to [the] inexperience [of] some principals who refer on simply to follow procedure only to find out later that the story was made up. But what can you do then? The person's life is already put in turmoil. I have seen teachers go with students and they have been punished, but I have also seen at least five allegations of molestation against teachers, both male and female, in the last three years [that] turned out to be fabricated . . .
>
> Principal 2, England, female

Principals have to make difficult decisions daily, many of which are based on judgement. The tension between judgement and procedure is a real one that further highlights the difficult nature of a principal's role. Nevertheless, inasmuch as principals should not be 'trigger happy', they were agreed that the safer thing to do, in the interest of all stakeholders, is to 'err on the side of caution', and report a concern 'they feel uncomfortable about' which itself is a decision based on judgement!

Reflection

Between April 2009 and March 2010, there were 2,827 accusations of abuse against teachers and 1,709 against non-teaching staff, more than half related to allegations of physical abuse in England (DfE/York Consulting Group, 2012). It remains unclear how many of these allegations turned out to be true or false. Nevertheless, the fact these allegations have been made presents principals with several challenges. How do schools keep students safe? How do schools attract male teachers? How do schools attract minority ethnic teachers? How do principals 'sell' their schools as 'safe' environments? These questions are as evocative as they are provocative. Successful and effective entrepreneurial principals who are also concerned about the health and safety of students should also consider these questions, and others, in light of what they are trying to achieve for their schools, putting students at the heart of what they do. Drawing on notions of entrepreneurialism in education (Hall & Southworth, 1997) and entrepreneurial leadership (Roomi & Harrison, 2011), I summarize the key skills and behaviours of entrepreneurial principals as being able to:

- recognize and analyse driving forces in the political, economic, social and technological environments in which they operate and understand the impact of these forces on their current strategies;
- develop winning strategies based on sound competitive analysis;
- understand the changing needs of students and be responsive to their expectations;
- involve others in strategy formulation and implementation;
- evaluate events and make strategic adjustments as needed;
- build for the future by increasing individual, interpersonal and organizational capacity.

As Gandz (2005) points out, 'There are two options, and both are good. The first is that I have knowhow as an architect; the second is how I can use this knowhow . . . to create wealth' (p. 61). Principals cannot take risks with safety and security decisions. And there can be no trade-off with safeguarding and child protection issues. Principals are continually being called to a higher performance bar on which they must balance entrepreneurial leadership with safety leadership in a way the keeps their school visible for the right reasons.

8

Evaluation, Implications and Conclusions

School leadership is what you get on the day. Some days it's evolutionary and you can reflect on the theory of leadership. Some days it's revolutionary and has nothing to do with what you've been taught or what you've learnt. In fact, there are days when you simply have to 'throw out the book', because school leadership is not black and white and no two days are alike.

Principal 8, Jamaica, female

When the school is functioning at its best, it comes into its own and does what it is supposed to do. It's outstanding; not only according to the judgement of inspectors, but based on its own judgement of itself. In other words, it self-actualizes. And self-actualizing will be the experience of everyone at all levels within the school. In this school however, resources are adequate and appropriate, leadership is shared and policy implementation carefully managed.

Principal 2, England, female

Introduction

A number of themes and issues have emerged from the data and case studies presented in this book. In trying to make sense of these, I have set out this concluding chapter in three sections. Section one presents an evaluation of the policy context of education through the 'economic-motor' metaphor I used in Chapter 6, but which I wish to develop and expand here. Section two considers and examines more closely the actual experiences of school principals through the leadership literature. In section three, key ideas from sections one and two are combined in the final section to highlight significant insights and to draw conclusions associated with the data presented in this book.

Evaluation

Global and national policy contexts impact the content, delivery and quality of education students receive, no matter where they live in a country or what country they live in. The policy context is necessary for social and international order to be maintained, although the management of policy implementation challenges this notion. More and more, education is being treated as a 'market good', to be bought, sold and provided to the 'highest bidder' and not the public merit good it used to be (and is supposed to be), accessible to everyone in equal quality and measure. In Chapter 6, I used the economic-motor metaphor to describe this situation, highlighting that governments around the world have positioned education/schooling as the 'panacea' to society's problems of economic growth and development. Growth (or development) is the outcome of education; education is the engine (or tool) of growth; the government is the owner and narrator of the policies; technocrats and policy officials are policy dispensers; the policies represent fuel and/or a roadmap; school principals are the drivers; teachers are the mechanics; and students represent the different parts of the vehicle.

As governments continue to more closely associate education and schooling with economic rather than social development, I use this metaphor to evaluate the work and experiences of school principals in an economically motivated educational context. This model should be thought of as an early stage or baseline model.

Government (policy-owners and narrators)

Governments have a legal duty to provide education to citizens of a country consistent with their ability to do so. This legal duty is affirmed in Article 26 of the UDHR, Article 13 of the International Covenant on Economic, Cultural and Social Rights (ICECSR) and Articles 28 and 29 of the UNCRC. In emphasizing the critical role of education/schooling in national development, the UN and associated agencies use catchphrases such as 'education beats poverty', 'education is not only a right but a passport to human development' and 'education opens doors and expands opportunities and freedoms'. It is the responsibility of a government to create the context and framework in which education/schooling can be provided to and accessed by citizens, and governments do this through the policies they develop and implement. Of note, governments own the policies and dictate their content, and in most countries they decide the curriculum students should pursue, the number of years of compulsory schooling, the number of years and programme content of initial teacher training, the number of contact days in a school/academic year, and whether education should be free to users or subsidized.

Technocrats and policy officials (policy dispensers)

Technocrats could be described as policy dispensers or 'henchmen'. As used here, henchmen are trusted supporters and advocates of a cause – in this case, government policies and their successful implementation. They do not own the policy but their primary duty is to get approval for and acceptance of government policy from users/groups, some way, somehow. The main concern of the henchmen/policy dispenser is getting a policy through and they have little or no concern for individual contexts or specificities of contexts. In a sense, they are rather like a service station attendant whose duty it is to 'pump' or 'sell' the fuel (in this case the actual policy) to drivers (in this case school principals).

The relationship between technocrats/policy officials (policy dispensers) and principals (drivers) has not always been smooth. Gunter (2012) describes this as a 'game to play where those outside of schools ... controlled the leadership of schools' (p. 18) and where 'the interplay between the agency of the headteacher and the structures that enable and prevent that agency' (Gunter, 2005, p. 172) are almost always at a crossroads. Furthermore, as Bell and Stevenson (2006, p. 44) ask, 'How does state policy manifest itself? The tools of policy are of course not value-neutral, and the way in which particular policies are enacted in particular contexts is intensely political ... policies cannot be disconnected from the socio-political environment within which they are framed'. These arguments highlight some 'theoretical and perspectival and ethical challenges that need further consideration ... the values and commitments of organisations and actors' (Ball, 2011, p. 52), and have led Eacott (2011) to assert that the current policy context is steadily leading to 'the cultural re-engineering of school leadership and the embedding of performativity in the leaders' soul' (p. 47).

Policies (fuel, roadmap)

As I discussed in Chapter 5 and elsewhere in this book, the policy context of education provides direction to and has a direct impact on what goes on in schools. Put differently, educational policies are the fuel on which education/ schooling is run, simultaneously establishing parameters and providing direction. In other words, no vehicle, no matter how expensive, no matter how well polished, is able to move without fuel. In Chapter 5, one Jamaican principal described a 'whirlwind of policies' that made it difficult for her to 'catch her breath' and to 'breathe'. Educational policies give shape and structure to an education system and can lead to both coherence and mayhem for those who must enforce, deliver or otherwise experience them. In the United Kingdom, for example, 'Since the 1988 Education Reform Act, under the leadership of different political administrations, there has been great centralisation' (Rayner, 2014, p. 38) and control despite the rhetoric of choice and school diversity (Bottery, 2007; Holligan et al., 2006).

As England's and Jamaica's education systems become more performativity based, 'School leaders have become sceptical of the notion of local autonomy because of an architecture of compliance within which their role is to define and meet performance targets' (Stoker, 2006, p. 44). This is certainly the case in both contexts, although more so in the UK where, until 2010, a fairly decentralized model of schooling was in place, which has since been replaced by a hybrid model of part centralized, part decentralized. Within what was a fairly decentralized system, however, existed a culture of 'close monitoring' by the state through school inspections and other performativity measures. As Thomson (2010, p. 9) asserts, 'Over less than a decade, English heads gained new freedoms and authorities to act within their schools, but there were also new audit and risk management procedures and new lines of accountability that delimited what could be done.'

These challenges to schools brought about by the policy context (fuel) are not confined to England and Jamaica. In Australia, Addison (2009) found the discourse and values of the business sector influenced organizational practice for and within schools even if they were in conflict with the values of those who led them. In this book I provide examples of principals consciously filtering policies, deciding against those they felt were unrealistic for where they were in their development and/or those for which they had no resources to implement, choosing instead to focus on those they could implement. In trying to provide students with the best educational experience possible, it appears principals have been caught up in a much bigger '... game in which market-based economic imperatives have become central to both their professional success and leadership practice' (Addison, 2009, p. 335), a game where they must learn a set of rules 'couched in economic language and with frequent intervention, or interference, from those beyond education' (Eacott, 2011, p. 50).

Principals (drivers)

School principals are arguably the most important group in the success or failure of schools and therefore in the success and/or failure of individuals and/or national development. A principal's ability to lead and therefore a principal's effectiveness is a function of several factors including quality and type of training received, their ongoing professional development, support from inside and outside the school, leadership characteristics and approach to leadership, and experience in teaching and leadership (and latterly, experience in marketing, budgeting and procurement).

In their theory of situated leadership, Miller and Hutton (2014) argue that effective school leadership is 'situated' within an individual but emerges from how they engage with and manage, negotiate and navigate internal and external factors. In other words, leadership is a function of external and internal factors, or $L = f(Ef + If)$, where: L = leadership practice; Ef = external factors; If = internal factors. They identified external factors including laws, policies, culture, school size and type, staff qualifications and experience and school location, along with internal factors including personal ability, socialization skills, experience, ambition, passion, commitment and enthusiasm.

Miller and Hutton propose that external factors (Ef) contextualize or set parameters for the practice of leadership whereas internal factors (If) deconstruct, interpret and engage external factors, thereby giving meaning to them, but in a personal and individual way. They argue, 'The practice of leadership, although constrained by external factors is essentially situated within an individual who must mediate external influences and factors through lenses that are personal and internal to the individual leader' (p. 88). In order for factors in the external environment, compounded by a fast-paced and sometimes conflictful policy environment, to be effective, and to deliver the type of education they believe their students should receive, principals will challenge and mediate external factors, where possible, to the benefit of their schools. In other words, principals are the 'drivers' of government policy at the operational level, and they do this in relation to their school's context, their vision for the school, the resources available to the school and in relation to where the school is currently 'at'.

In drawing on foundations in their personal and professional pasts (Hall & Southworth, 1997), Jamaican and English principals engaged in 'policy filtering' and 'policy re-interpreting', as they saw fit, taking personal and professional risks as they tried to ensure students' time at school was beneficial to them in line with government guidelines and local contexts. This view of principals having to use government policy as fuel to take a different path to get to the prescribed end-point perhaps underlines Peters and Waterman's (1982) view of them as 'the mover of the mission' and the 'manager of the boundary' (p. 143). Nevertheless, some principals felt they were merely facilitating a process of schooling where the outcomes and contexts had been determined by the government.

Teachers (mechanics)

Teachers are foundational to a successful system of schooling. Through their skills, knowledge and experience they provide students with the skills they need in order to function effectively and independently in society. Teaching is 'an ethic of care' (Smith, 2011, p. 529). As a result, and consistent with the policy context (fuel, road map) and the vision, directive and support of the principal (driver), teachers work to enable students (different parts of a vehicle) through education (tools: the curriculum knowledge and related skills through teaching, assessment and feedback). Article 28 of the UNCRC 1989 requires 'States Parties [to] recognize the right of the child to education'. Article 29 extends 28 by outlining the aims and objectives of the type and quality of education a child receives.

States Parties agree that the education of the child shall be directed to:

(a) The development of the child's personality, talents and mental and physical abilities to their fullest potential;

(b) The development of respect for human rights and fundamental freedoms, and for the principles enshrined in the Charter of the United Nations;

(c) The development of respect for the child's parents, his or her own cultural identity, language and values, for the national values of the country in which the child is living, the country from which he or she may originate, and for civilizations different from his or her own;

(d) The preparation of the child for responsible life in a free society, in the spirit of understanding, peace, tolerance, equality of sexes, and friendship among all peoples, ethnic, national and religious groups and persons of indigenous origin;

(e) The development of respect for the natural environment.

It is teachers (mechanics) who are tasked with making an education system function through delivering the agreed or prescribed curriculum in line with other national and/or international policy guidelines. As a result, the principal's critical role in recruiting, deploying and developing staff is once more highlighted. Furthermore, the role of teachers and other staff in contributing to national development outcomes (economic growth) is manifest.

Students (different parts of a vehicle)

Students are the reason why schools and other educational institutions exist. They come from varying backgrounds, they represent different racial/ethnic groups, they have varying needs and serve as ambassadors for many different religious and cultural groups. Due to their diversity, they provide teachers (mechanics), schools, and therefore society with many challenges and opportunities, highlighting an active socializing and symbiotic relationship in which, although being moulded, they contribute actively to the process of their own moulding.

Education (engine, tools)

Educational achievement and outcomes can and do have a positive effect on a country's economic growth. As the skills of a workforce increases and are utilized, worker productivity increases (Psacharopoulos & Patrinos, 2004; Patrinos et al., 2006). Professionals, including accountants, scientists, engineers, lawyers, nurses and teachers are produced by an educational system, and if these workers are not in good supply, economic growth could be threatened. As a result, governments are interested in students going to schools and being provided with education. Put another way, the more schooling one has, the greater one's chances of success and therefore the greater likelihood of a greater contribution to national economic development (Schultz, 1963).

Rivera-Batiz (2008) proposes that a key reason some countries have been unable to grow their educational system, despite expanding educational provision, is due to the low quality of their schooling. It is not clear whether in this case years of schooling is associated with the quality of schooling or, rather, what is taught, how it is taught and how it is assessed. Nevertheless, as countries increase the quantity of schooling, if the quality schooling is low, or if it is in decline, then expected results for students and the economy may not be delivered. As Lee (1999, p. 16) notes, 'Human capital is considered one of the major factors in explaining ... economic growth'.

Whereas students' enrolment may be increasing, if the quality of education provided to and received by students is poor, then the knowledge acquired, the cognitive skills developed and therefore the qualifications gained may offer only limited or no real opportunities. Dugger (2004, p. 10) notes that 'just herding kids into classes and calling that education hasn't worked'. If the quantity and quality of schooling are in place, through an inclusive and balanced curriculum that allows for the development of higher cognitive skills, through adequate classroom space, and material and equipment, and if adequate support structures are available to and are in schools, then the expectations for productivity and economic growth can be significant.

Growth/development (outcomes of education)

Education's role in national development is much debated in terms of its social or economic outcomes. Education is a public good, but it is also a merit good. As a merit good, the role and value of schooling does not end with the education a person receives but has a role to play, for example, in crime and unemployment reduction, revenue generation and increasing a country's gross domestic product (GDP).

The World Bank believes that 'Education is critical for economic growth and poverty reduction ... Investment in education contributes to the accumulation of human capital, which is essential for higher incomes and sustained economic growth' (1995, p. 1). Furthermore, Lucas (1993, p. 270) proposes that 'The main engine of growth is the accumulation of human capital – of knowledge – and the main source of differences in living standards among nations is differences in human capital'. Recent studies (Bosworth & Collins, 2003; Rivera-Batiz, 2007) have also found a positive relationship between increased educational attainment and economic growth – a relationship that governments are keen to 'exploit' through schooling, and especially in light of ongoing challenges in the global economic environment. Once more, the implications for a school principal are clear: the road to national economic development starts at the gate of a school. Below, I summarize the different parts of the metaphor I have used above into a baseline model which I describe as the economic-motor model of schooling (see Figure 8.1).

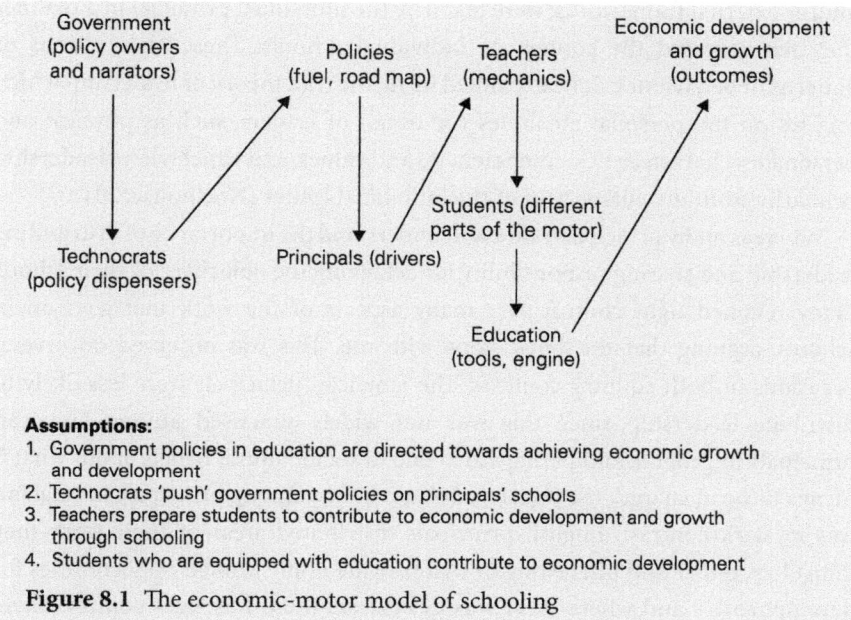

Assumptions:
1. Government policies in education are directed towards achieving economic growth and development
2. Technocrats 'push' government policies on principals' schools
3. Teachers prepare students to contribute to economic development and growth through schooling
4. Students who are equipped with education contribute to economic development

Figure 8.1 The economic-motor model of schooling

Implications

In addition to the policy implications as set out above, the experiences of principals also point to a number of implications about a principal's work. I have grouped the main implications into four main categories: leadership is situated, work/role intensification, the intensity of leadership and the paradox of leadership. In discussing these, I draw on, and link these, to Northouse's (2012, pp. 6–8) definition of leadership as: traits, skills, behaviour, relationships and influence. In what follows leadership is situated (is linked to traits); work/role intensification (is linked to skills); the intensity of leadership (is linked to behaviours); and the paradox of leadership (is linked to influence and relationships). I discuss these in turn below.

Leadership is situated (traits)

An important observation among principals in this study was the 'individuality' of leadership. That is, many of the tasks they had to do could only be done by them, and many of these tasks were completed alone, often in isolation due to time and other constraints. Similarly, many decisions taken, despite internal and/or external frameworks, were taken by the individual principal in a manner they felt reflected the context of individual schools. These observations of patterns of behaviour can be explained using the trait theory of leadership which focuses on the personal attributes (or traits) of leaders, such as physical and personality characteristics, competencies and values, and which views leadership primarily from the perspective of the individual leader (Northouse, 2012).

Whereas many principals know and understand the importance of distributing leadership and sharing responsibility for achieving the objectives of their school, many retained tight control over many aspects of the work that goes on in schools, arguing that the 'buck stops with me'. This was observed on several occasions in both country contexts. The Jamaican principals were less likely to distribute leadership since this was not widely practised among Jamaican principals in general, and perhaps also due to sociocultural beliefs about what it means to 'be in charge'. The pattern of observations among principals in England was in stark contrast. English principals distributed areas of their work they didn't like, didn't find interesting or that provided only limited opportunities for development – and where there was delegation, there was tight control. There was only limited evidence of what could be described as genuine or real distributed leadership. Nevertheless, what has emerged from these observations, among both sets of principals, is a picture of principals who are in charge of their schools and who are committed to their job role. Although principals tended to retain control of their school's budget, it is not clear whether they 'had to' be in charge of many other tasks as well or whether they simply 'felt they had to be'. Research in this area could be useful in helping to understand principals' decision-making and the role of traits in decision-making. It was clear that principals in this case study were committed, decisive, competent, courageous and assertive.

Work/role intensification (skills)

Northouse (2012) considers leadership to be a skill, a form of balancing act, and by necessity, a prerequisite for effective school leadership. Not only are principals being called upon to demonstrate skills in leadership, more and more they are called upon to demonstrate skills in several other job-related roles. Work and role intensification was a major issue among all principals. On the one hand, work intensification had come to mean 'longer working hours', 'earlier starts', 'more meetings' and 'late nights'. On the other hand, role intensification had come to mean 'jack of all trades', 'counsellor', 'psychologist', 'security guard', 'teacher', 'teaching assistant', 'cook', 'lunchtime supervisor', 'cleaner', 'police' and 'inventory clerk'.

In larger schools, principals appeared to have constructed their roles along three interrelated lines:

- **judge:** leader; decision-maker; interpreter of standards; symbol and source of authority and knowledge; resourcer; interpreter, keeper and driver of rules and policies;
- **juror:** weigher of evidence; maker of judgements; disturbance-handler; screener and sifter of information and facts;
- **executioner:** enforcer of policies and rules; disciplinarian; dispenser of justice; monitor of quality and service standards.

In smaller schools, principals seemingly occupied the three roles associated with principals in larger schools. But they also seemingly occupied several additional roles. Whereas all principals faced work intensification, principals in larger schools were in a better position to spread their work since better and more organized systems of support were available to them. Role intensification among principals of smaller and rural/remote schools was a noticeable issue.

Hughes (1995) constructed the role of the principal as a business function concerned primarily with the allocation of resources, coordination of events, professional guidance and development of staff, teaching and learning, along with relationship management. The changing nature of school leadership has meant a simultaneous threat to and the expansion of these roles – challenging the status and role of the 'master teacher' and 'lead practitioner'. The current education context in both Jamaica and England requires principals to acquire and demonstrate new skills, as it were, to keep their schools open and therefore their jobs, reinforcing Eacott's (2011) notion that the (current) policy context is steadily leading to 'the cultural re-engineering of school leadership and the embedding of performativity in the leaders' soul' (p. 47).

Intensity of leadership (behaviours)

'Intensity' was an observable behavioural trait among principals. Northouse's (2102) definition of leadership also has a focus on behaviours. In this study, 'intensity' is used to mean a positive value such as being focused, determined, passionate or highly motivated. All principals showed intense leadership in how they did their jobs, although this was more noticeable in some areas.

Principals were clear they are leading in a time of competition and rapid change where 'relevance' is an enduring characteristic of a school. They 'sold' their school, highlighting positives from staff experience and qualifications, safety record, and subjects offered. By treating staff with respect, by involving them in decision-making and by motivating them through supporting their interests and professional development, principals were more likely to realize their visions for their schools. They also positioned themselves as capable, motivated, committed, trustworthy, courageous and unwavering in the face of ongoing challenges.

> There is no other job I want to do. I love seeing the kids thrive and do well. If I could give them another 10 years, but I can't . . . I am getting on in age.
>
> Principal 10, Jamaica, female

> Sometimes I am so fed up with parents, with teachers, with the Department for Education . . . but when I get like that, I know I am tired and need a couple hours' sleep, after which I'll be back to normal.
>
> Principal 6, England, male

There was an inescapable sense of intense commitment to students, staff, school communities and national development that enabled principals to want to keep going in the face of challenges, setbacks, disappointment and sometimes even disillusionment. A major factor explaining effective school leadership within the framework of situated leadership is commitment, which is an important personal factor. According to Miller and Hutton (2014), when enthusiasm is applied to commitment this increases the intensity of leadership and leads to more effective leadership. It is this intensity of leadership that makes principals offer themselves up daily, almost as sacrificial lambs, to the cause of national development through education in the hope they'll contribute to transforming the lives and futures of students and their families. Intensity quickens in the face of adversity and uncertainty, is resilient, is determined and is persevering – demanding that principals 'try new things', and try to 'find a way' that delivers the best possible educational experience and outcomes for students and their families. Observable patterns of behaviour among principals were determination, risk-taking and entrepreneurialism, supporting staff development, protecting the time of staff from distraction, networking and collaboration, which I consider central and proprietal roles of a school principal.

The paradox of leadership (relationships/influence)

The paradox of leadership was another observable theme among principals. In other words, a principal's role and the 'status' as perceived by others on the 'outside' was not always the reality. The ability to influence others and build/ sustain relationships is an element of effective leadership (Northouse, 2012).

Nearly all principals shared a degree of anxiety due to an event that had occurred or was about to occur, or in relation to a decision that had been taken or was to be taken. One principal used the phrase, 'stomach turning' to describe the anxiety she felt when examination results were to be released. Judgment was crucial to their role and some spoke of 'weighing up all the issues' before making certain decisions, especially regarding procurement, disciplinary matters and/or employment termination. To an outsider, a principal's job is 'easy' or clear-cut: moving students from point A to point B. To an aspiring principal, the behind the scenes workings and demands of a principal's role will only fully come alive at or after their appointment, although shadowing should provide some useful insights. Principals described being an actual school leader as very different from what they'd imagined it to be. They spoke candidly of feelings of isolation with no one to turn to for help, and of feeling incompetent, unsure and vulnerable. These descriptions of their own work reflect a 'living contradiction' (Whitehead, 1985, p. 10).

Despite the contradictions, principals fully understood and accepted their role in leading change at the school level and in contributing to change at a societal level. There was some tension about how much they could support, or should be expected to support other neighbouring schools in order to bolster their own improvement. Their apprehension was not due to any lack of understanding about the role of education in society's development; rather, it was because some feared being 'distracted' by efforts to support others at the expense of their own school since, 'I am being judged only for the success or failure of my school ... so I cannot afford to be side-tracked'. In Chapter 7, I described the practice of principals consciously refusing to support weaker schools in their education zones as an 'inverted view of systems leadership'. This view is understandably shaped by and intertwined with notions of performativity and accountability as principals become more calculated in how, why and to whom they reach out. Further research on how notions of performativity impact a principal's ability or willingness to work with other (weaker) schools may provide an understanding of the breadth and depth of these behaviours and issues.

Conclusions

Constant changes in a school's policy environment, underpinned by increased workload and the need to guarantee national economic development, have left principals feeling vulnerable and isolated. As far back as 1995, Southworth reported that, 'school leaders ... are under tighter pressure now more than ever to act quickly' (p. 199). This is still the case today. Principals showed great resilience and courage although showing signs of frustration and anxiety due to external pressures and the positioning of schooling as *the* route to national economic growth and development.

The professional development of principals is a most important issue for governments. Underlining this fact, Jamaican education minister, Revd Ronald Thwaites told fellow parliamentarians on 13 January 2015,

> Last year, the [National] College [for Educational Leadership] trained 1,270 school leaders in a number of critical areas to improve student performance ... the National Education Inspectorate found that 57 per cent of schools assessed up to June 2014 were rated as satisfactory and above in leadership and management. A little more than 43 per cent were deemed to be unsatisfactory ... In addition to on-the-job training for educators in positions of leadership, NCEL is also preparing prospective principals through the Aspiring Principals Programme (APP).
>
> Gleaner, 2015

In a speech in February 2015, British Prime Minister David Cameron expressed concerns about leadership and the performance of schools (BBC, 2015). Citing data from Ofsted which showed nearly a quarter of secondary schools, about 720, and 2,600 primary schools recently inspected were described as 'requiring improvement' he said,

> No one wants their child to go to a failing school and no one wants to them to go to a coasting school either ... 'Just enough' is not good enough. That means no more sink schools and no more 'bog standard' schools either ... Our aim is this: the best start in life for every child, wherever they're from – no excuses.

For schools to (continue to) improve, and for society to be best placed to contribute to the outcomes of education, as constructed by politicians, principal development must be taken seriously and pressure must be met with support. Principals based in rural and remote communities were less likely to access professional development opportunities, due to having no relief or due to staffing issues. People leadership is serious business, and the development of the 'driver' of the vehicle whose outcome is economic growth and development can only be seen as a sensible investment.

Principals are finding it harder to balance work and family commitments and some (four) confirmed their demanding workload had caused 'problems at home'. One described 'missing so many important milestones in the life of my children' and another conceded that 'even at weekends and during school holidays I am working . . . there is no let-up'. School events, meeting with parents, meetings of the board, disciplinary hearings, meetings at the education department/ministry, had consumed them. They also talked of being 'constantly tired' due to meetings and paperwork, and also due to their day-to-day involvement in operational matters at school. In 1996, Webb and Vulliamy (1996) reported, '. . . because of constant interruptions to the head's work schedule it is extremely difficult during the school day to achieve the work planned, which resulted in the bulk of it being taken home after school and a build-up of tasks to be tackled in the holidays' (p. 305). Boyle and Woods (1996) also argue that due to workload, 'the familial role gets squeezed', with some principals not being able to 'find time to cook for their children . . .' (p. 562).

Principals are operating in a time of increased scrutiny and increased accountability. They are also operating in a time where competition between schools, competition between school systems, performativity, public accountability, naming and shaming of schools, high-stakes testing and standards have become the new norm. In line with this, Eacott urges principals to 'engage in conversations of the world' and to contribute to 'robust research that engages with the complexity of school leadership practice' (2011, p. 51).

The data from conversations with 10 school principals in Jamaica and England, two very different schooling contexts, have helped us to understand, and more so appreciate, how consistently challenging school leadership is and can be. The conversations have helped us to identify the traits these principals have developed over time and why they lead the way they do. Likewise, the conversations have helped us to identify what Bogue (1985) calls the enemies of leadership: ignorance, prejudice, rigidity, apathy, indecision, mediocrity, imitation, arrogance, inefficiency and duplicity. Three decades on from Bogue, the enemies of leadership as he described them are still prevalent today. Nevertheless, in the context of school leadership, and in the context of this book, the enemies of school leadership could be construed as a volatile policy environment, work intensification, a culture of performativity, accountability through inspections, standards-based testing, performance league tables and the naming and shaming of schools that are in need of support.

The conversations and observations also highlighted and affirmed several important qualities and approaches to school leadership: vision, justice, commitment, passion, trust, hard work, judgement and being conceptually skilled, trait leadership, transactional leadership, visionary leadership, transformative leadership, distributed leadership, transformational leadership and servant leadership. Principals also showed:

- adaptability and openness to change;
- self-awareness and emotional intelligence;
- awareness of their leadership strengths and areas for development;
- resilience and courage;
- vision and strategic thinking;
- awareness of the 'business' environment and the implications for schools;
- creativity and appreciation of forms of partnership working.

The principals in this study showed there was no one 'best way' to lead, but that their approach to leadership was related to their abilities, context (school, cultural, national), prevailing environmental factors and the abilities of followers. They cast themselves as 'servant leaders', in service to students, their families, staff, school communities and country.

Throughout my several conversations with the principals, they often associated thought with action. Without the test of action, according to Bezzina et al. (2003) 'a decision was sterile and empty' (p. 206). Principals showed a high level of moral commitment, although not without difficulties or dilemmas. Although principals were different in terms of personality, education, background, gender, culture and country context, they all showed a common pattern of devotion to those principles cherished, valued and modelled by the school leader who leads with integrity (Wasserberg, 1999). Between England and Jamaica, the stories and experiences of principals present new voices in the debate on school leadership practice, and new perspectives, highlighting more similarities than differences in terms of structures, agency and effectiveness. There was a demonstrable pattern of psychological determination among the principals that, although acknowledging the challenges they were up against, also shed light on their character and on their beliefs about their role in individual, school and national development.

A final observation from my conversations with principals is the important link between leadership and learning. While this may seem obvious, the concept of learning, as expressed here, means more than seeking new qualifications. Principals wanted more time to be engaged in individual and collective reflection and also to be able to participate in professional development activities that would enable them to more appropriately situate and interrogate their practice and also to help them become better at what they do. Principals constantly and actively challenged their attitudes and behaviours towards education, schooling, their leadership and the national policy context – highlighting how these behaviours and attitudes were as problematic in leadership and leading as the volatility of the policy environment.

Appendix
Profile of Principals

Case study	P1 Tom	P2 Kerry	P3 Jane	P4 Mary	P5 Tony	P6 Dave	P7 Mike	P8 Erica	P9 Edith	P10 Trudy
Gender	M	F	F	F	M	M	M	F	F	F
Approximate age	45	36	38	36	55	45	45	45	43	53
Teaching experience	18	10	10	10	25	18	20	15	12	27
Principal experience (years)	12	2	8	5	16	8	13	2	1	8
Principal experience (schools)	1	2	1	1	3	2	2	1	2	1
Years in current post	5	2	8	5	6	1	1	1	1	8
Country	UK	UK	JA	JA	UK	UK	UK	JA	UK	JA
In-country location	Suburban	Inner-city	Rural	Remote	Urban	Inner-city	Urban	Rural	Urban	Inner-city
School type	Suburban High Academy	East London High	Remote Primary One – Jamaica	Remote Primary Two – Jamaica	Outer London High	Inner London Primary	University High	Jamaica Primary	West London High	Inner-city Primary

References

Acker, S. (1990). Managing the drama: the headteacher's work in an urban primary school. Paper presented at a Conference on Histories and Ethnographies of Teachers at Work, Oxford.

Addison, B. (2009). A feel for the game – a Bourdieuian analysis of principal leadership: a study of Queensland secondary school principals, *Journal of Educational Administration and History*, 41(4), pp. 327–41.

Adler, N. J. & Bartholomew, S. (1992). Managing globally competent people, *Academy of Management Executive*, 6, pp. 52–65.

Afshari, M., Bakar, K., Luan, W., Samah, B. & Fooi, F. (2009). Technology and school leadership. *Technology, Pedagogy and Education,* 18(2), pp. 235–48.

Ainscow, M., Booth, T. & Dyson, A., with Farrell, P., Frankham, J., Gallannaugh, F., Howes, A. & Smith, R. (2006). *Improving Schools, Developing Inclusion*. London: Routledge.

Alexander, R., Rose, J. & Woodhead, C. (1992). *Curriculum Organisation and Classroom Practice: a discussion paper*. London: DES.

Anderson, R. & Dexter, S. (2005). School technology leadership: an empirical investigation of prevalence and effect, *Educational Administration Quarterly*, 41(1), pp. 49–82.

Armstrong, A. C., Armstrong, D. & Spandagou, I. (2010). *Inclusive Education: International Policy & Practice*. London: Sage.

Armstrong, D., Armstrong, A. C. & Spandagou, I. (2011). Inclusion: by choice or by chance? *International Journal of Inclusive Education*, 15(1), pp. 29–39.

Arnot, M. & Gelsthorpe, L. (2010). *Education, Asylum and the 'Non-Citizen' Child: The Politics of Comparison and Belonging*. London: Palgrave Macmillan.

Assessment Reform Group (1999). *Assessment for Learning: Beyond the Black Box*. Cambridge: University of Cambridge School of Education.

Atkinson, J. M. & Heritage, J. (1984). *Structures of Social Action: Studies in Conversation Analysis*. Cambridge: Cambridge University Press.

Atwater, D. & Bass, B. M. (1994). Transformational leadership in teams, in B. M. Bass and B. Avolio (eds) *Improving Organizational Effectiveness through Transformational Leadership*. Thousand Oaks, CA: Sage Publications.

Avery, D. C. (2005). *Understanding Leadership*. London: Sage.

Awalt, C. & Jolly, D. (1999). An inch deep and a mile wide: electronic tools for savvy administrators, *Educational Technology & Society*, 2(3), pp. 97–105.

Bailey, G. D. (1997). What technology leaders need to know: the essential top 10 concepts for technology integration in the 21st century? *Learning & Leading with Technology*, 25(1), pp. 57–62.

Balarin, M., Brammer, S., James, C. & McCormack, M. (2008). *Governing our Schools: a Research Study Commissioned by Business in the Community.* London: BITC.

Ball, S. (1987). *The Micro-politics of the School: Towards a Theory of School Organization.* London: Routledge.

Ball, S., Maguire, M., Braun, A. & Hoskins, K. (2011). Policy actors: doing policy work in schools, *Discourse: Studies in the Cultural Politics of Education,* 32(4), pp. 625–39.

Ball, S. J. (2011). A new research agenda for educational leadership and policy, *Management in Education,* 25(2), pp. 50–2.

Ball, S. J. (2012). *Global Education Inc. New Policy Networks and the Neo-Liberal Imaginary.* Abingdon: Routledge.

Bass, B. (1981). *Stogdill's Handbook of Leadership Revised.* New York: Free Press.

BBC (2015). Cameron challenged on 'no cuts' school funding promise. 2nd February. Available at: http://www.bbc.co.uk/news/education-31087137.

Bell, L. & Stevenson, H. (2006). *Education Policy: Process, themes and impact.* London: RoutledgeFalmer.

Bezzina, C., Cassar, V. & Triganza-Scott, A. (2003). *Educational Leaders in the Making.* Malta: Indigo Books.

Bhavani, R., Mirza, H. & Meetoo, V. (2005). *Tackling the Roots of Racism: Lessons for Success.* Bristol: The Policy Press.

Blasé, J. & Anderson, G. (1995). *The Micropolitics of Educational Leadership: From control to empowerment.* London: Cassell.

Blow, L., Goodman, A., Walker, I. & Windmeijer, F. (2005). *Parental Background and Child Outcomes: Does money matter and what else matters? DfES Research Report 660.* London: DfES.

Boal, K. B. & Hooijberg, R. (2001). Strategic leadership research: moving on, *Leadership Quarterly,* 11(4): pp. 515–49.

Bogue, G. (1985). *The Enemies of Leadership: Lessons for leaders in education.* Arlington, VA: Phi Delta Kappa Educational Foundation.

Bolman, L. G. & Heller, R. (1995). Research on school leadership: the state-of-the-art. In S. B. Bacharach & B. Mundell (eds), *Images of Schools: Structures and roles in organizational behavior.* California: Corwin Press Inc.

Bosworth, B. & Collins, S. (2003). *The Empirics of Growth: An update.* Brookings Papers on Economic Activity. No. 1.

Bottery, M. (2007). Reports from the front line: English headteachers' work in an era of practice centralization, *Educational Management Administration & Leadership,* 35(1), pp. 89–110.

Bowe, R. & Ball, S. J. with Gold, A. (1992). *Reforming Education and Changing Schools.* London: Routledge.

Boyle, M. & Woods, P. (1996). The composite head: coping with changes in the primary headteacher's role, *British Educational Research Journal,* 22(5), pp. 549–68.

Brighouse, T. (2006). *On Education,* Abingdon: Routledge.

Brighouse, T. (2007). *How Successful Headteachers Survive and Thrive: Four phases of headship, five uses of time, six essential tasks and seven ways to hold on to your sanity.* London: RM Education.

Brockmeier, L. L., Sermon, J. M. & Hope, W. C. (2005). Principal's relationship with computer technology, *NASSP Bulletin*, 89(643), pp. 45–63.

Brown, G. (2005). *The Hugo Young Memorial Lecture.* Chatham House, December 13.

Brown, G. (2010). Gordon Brown: 'This election will be about social mobility'. Speech given to the Fabian Society New Year Conference, January.

Brown, L. & Lavia, J. (2013). School leadership and inclusive education in Trinidad & Tobago: dilemmas and opportunities for practice. In P. Miller (ed.) *School Leadership in the Caribbean: perceptions, practices, paradigms.* London: Symposium Books.

Brown, L. I. & Conrad, D. (2007). School leadership in Trinidad and Tobago: the challenge of context, *Comparative Education Review*, 51(2), pp. 181–202.

Bubb, S. & Earley, P. (2007). *Leading and Managing Continuing Professional Development,* 2nd edn. London: Paul Chapman.

Bush, T. (2003). Theory and practice in educational management. In T. Bush, M. Coleman & M. Thurlow (eds) *Leadership & Strategic Management in South African Schools.* London: Commonwealth Secretariat.

Busher, H. (2006). *Understanding Educational Leadership: People, power and culture.* Maidenhead: Open University Press.

Busher, H. & Barker, B. (2003). The crux of leadership: shaping school culture by contesting the policy contexts and practices of teaching and learning, *Educational Management and Administration,* 31(1), pp. 51–65.

Cameron, D. (2007). *Social Responsibility: The big idea for Britain's future.* London: Conservative Party.

Carli, L. L. & Eagly, A. H. (2011). Gender and leadership. In A. Bryman, D. Collinson, K. Grint, B. Jackson and M. Uhl-Bien (eds) *The SAGE Handbook of Leadership.* London: Sage, pp. 103–17.

Carnoy, M. (2007). *Cuba's Academic Advantage: Why students in Cuba do better in school.* Stanford, CA: Stanford University Press.

Carnoy, M., Elmore, R. & Siskin, L. S. (eds) (2003). *The New Accountability: High schools and high-stakes testing.* New York: RoutledgeFalmer.

Chang, I-H. (2012). The effect of principals' technological leadership on teachers' technological literacy and teaching effectiveness in Taiwanese elementary schools, *Educational Technology & Society*, 15(2), pp. 328–40.

Chapman, C. & Harris, A. (2004). Improving schools in difficult and challenging contexts: strategies for improvement, *Educational Research*, 46(3), pp. 219–29.

Chief Secretary to the Treasury (2003). *Every Child Matters.* Norwich: The Stationery Office.

Chin, J. M. (2010). *Theory and Application of Educational Leadership.* Taipei, TW: Wunan.

Conger, J. (1992). *Learning to Lead: The art of transforming managers into leaders,* San Francisco, CA: Jossey-Bass.

Coulson, A. A. (1976). The role of the primary head. In T. Bush et al. (eds) *Approaches to School Management*. London: Harper & Row.

Coulson, A. A. (1986). *The Managerial Work of Primary School Headteachers*, Sheffield Papers in Education Management, No. 48, Sheffield, Sheffield City Polytechnic.

Craig, G. (2002). Ethnicity, citizenship and the labour market. In J. G. Andersen & P. Jensen (eds) *Citizenship, Welfare and the Labour Market*. Bristol: Policy Press.

Daft, R. L. (2011). The Leadership Experience, 5th edn. Westport, CT: Greenwood.

Dean, C., Dyson, A., Gallannaugh, F., Howes, A. & Raffo, C. (2007). *School Governors and Disadvantage*. London: Joseph Rowntree Foundation.

DEFRA (2012) *Statistical Digest of Rural England 2012*, https://www.gov.uk/government/uploads/system/uploads/attachment_data/file/69493/pb13642-rural-digest-2012.pdf.

den Hartog, D. N., House, R. J., Hanges, P. J., Ruiz-Quintanilla, S. A. & Dorfman, P. W. (1999). Culture specific and cross-culturally generalizable implicit leadership theories: are attributes of charismatic/transformational leadership universally endorsed? *Leadership Quarterly*, 10(12), pp. 219–56.

Department for Education/York Consulting Group (2012). *Allegations of Abuse Against Teachers and Non-teaching Staff*. Research Report DFE-RR192. West Yorkshire: York Consulting Group.

DfES (Department for Education and Skills) (2007). *Gender and Education: The evidence on pupils in England*. Nottingham: DfES, http://webarchive.nationalarchives.gov.uk/20130401151715/http://www.education.gov.uk/publications/eOrderingDownload/00389-2007BKT-EN.pdf.

Department for Education (2013). *Health and Safety: Advice on legal duties and powers for local authorities, school leaders, school staff and governing bodies*. London: DfE.

Dolby, N. (2012). *Rethinking Multicultural Education for the Next Generation: The new empathy and social justice*. New York: Routledge.

Drath, W. H. (2001). *The Deep Blue Sea: Rethinking the source of leadership*. San Francisco, CA: Jossey-Bass.

DuBrin, A. (2010). *Leadership: Research findings, practice and skills*, 6th edn. Mason, OH: South-Western/Cengage.

Dugger, C. (2004). In Africa, free schools feed a different hunger, *The New York Times*, 24 October, pp. 1, 10.

Dunphy, D. & Stace, D. (1988). Transformational and coercive strategies for planned organisational change, *Organization Studies*, 9(3), pp. 317–34.

Dzidonu, C. (2010). *The Role of ICTs to achieving the MDGs in Education: An analysis of the case of African countries*, commissioned paper, United Nations Department of Economic and Social Affairs (UNDESA).

Eacott, S. (2011). Preparing 'educational' leaders in managerialist times: an Australian story, *Journal of Educational Administration and History*, 43(1), pp. 43–59.

Eagly, A. & Carli, L. (2007). *Through the Labyrinth: The truth about how women become leaders*. Boston, MA: Harvard Business School Press.

Earley, P. (2013). Foreword. In P. Miller (ed.) *School Leadership in the Caribbean: Perceptions, practices, paradigms*. London: Symposium Books.

Earley, P., Evans, J., Collarbone, P., Gold, A. & Halpin, D. (2002). *Establishing the Current State of School Leadership in England*. Department for Education & Skills research report RR336. London: HMSO.

Earley, P., Higham, R., Allen, R., Allen, T., Howson, J., Nelson, R. & Sims, D. (2012). *Review of the School Leadership Landscape*. Nottingham: National College for School Leadership.

Edge, K., Frayman, K. and Jaafar, S. (2009). *North South School Partnerships: Learning from schools in the UK, Africa and Asia*. London, IoE.

Fabian Society (2006). *Narrowing the Gap: The Fabian Commission on life chances and children in poverty*. London: Fabian Society.

Farrell, G. (2007). *Survey of ICT in Education in Kenya*. Washington, DC: infoDev/World Bank.

Flanagan, L. & Jacobsen, M. (2003). Technology leadership for the twenty-first century principal, *Journal of Educational Administration*, 41(2), pp. 124–42.

Frost, D. & Durrant, J. (2003). Teacher leadership: rationale, strategy and impact, *School Leadership and Management*, 23(2), pp. 173–86.

Fullan, M. (1991). The meaning of educational change, in M. G. Fullan, *The New Meaning of Educational Change*. New York: Teachers College Press, pp. 30–46.

Fullan, M. (2001). *Leading in a Culture of Change*. San Francisco: Jossey-Bass.

Gandz, J. (2005). The leadership role, *Ivey Business Journal*, 66(1), p. 5.

Gardner, H. & Laskin, E. (1995). *Leading Minds: An anatomy of leadership*. New York: Basic Books.

Giddens, A. (1984). *The Constitution of Society: Outline of the Theory of Structuration*. Cambridge: Polity Press.

Glaser, B. G. & Strauss, A. L. (1976). *The Discovery of Grounded Theory. Strategies for qualitative research*. New Jersey: Aldine Transaction.

Gleaner (2015). New qualifications for principals coming, 14 January, http://jamaica-gleaner.com/gleaner/20150114/lead/lead2.html.

Goodlad, J. (2004). *A Place Called School*. New York: McGraw-Hill.

Gosmire, D. & Grady, M. (2007). *A Bumpy Road: Principal as technology leader*, https://www.nassp.org/portals/0/content/55193.pdf.

Grace, G. (1995). *School Leadership Beyond Education Management: An essay in policy scholarship*. London: Routledge.

Grace, G. (2001). St. Michael's Roman Catholic Comprehensive School. In M. Maden (ed.) *Success Against the Odds – Five Years On*. London: RoutledgeFalmer.

Grady, M. (2011a). *Leading the Technology Powered School*. Thousand Oaks, CA: Corwin.

Grady, M. (2011b). The principal's role as technology leader, http://seenmagazine.us/articles/article-detail/articleid/1800/the-principal%E2%80%99s-role-as-technology-leader.aspx.

Gray, J. (2001). Building for improvement and sustaining change in schools serving disadvantaged communities. In M. Maden (ed.) *Success Against the Odds – Five Years On*. London: RoutledgeFalmer.

Great Britain (1991). *Standards in Education: the annual report of HM Senior Chief Inspector of Schools based on the work of HMI in England*. London: DES.

Gronn, P. (2003). *The New Work of Educational Leaders: Changing leadership practice in an era of school reform*. London: Sage.

Gunter, H. M. (2005). Conceptualising research in educational leadership, *Educational Management Administration & Leadership*, 33(2), pp. 43–59.

Gunter, H. M. (2012). *Leadership and the Reform of Education*. Bristol: The Policy Press.

Haber, S. (2009). Why banks don't lend: the Mexican financial system. In S. Levy & M. Walton (eds) *No Growth without Equity? Inequality, interests, and competition in Mexico*. Washington, DC: The World Bank and Palgrave Macmillan.

Hall, V. & Southworth, G. (1997). Headship, school leadership & management, *School Organisation*, 17(2), pp. 152–70.

Hargreaves, A. (1994). *Changing Teachers, Changing Times: Teachers' work and culture in the post-modern age*. London: Cassell.

Harris, S. & Mixon, J. (eds) (2014). *Building Cultural Community through Global Educational Leadership*. Ypsilanti, MI: NCPEA Publications.

Harris, A. & Spillane, J. (2008). Distributed leadership through the looking glass, *Management in Education*, 22(31), pp. 31–4.

Hatcher, R. (2005). The distribution of leadership and power in schools, *British Journal of Sociology of Education*, 26(2), pp. 253–68.

Hattie, J. (2002). Why is it so difficult to enhance self-concept in the classroom: the power of feedback in the self-concept-achievement relationship. Paper presented at the conference for Self-Concept Research: Driving International Research Agendas, Sydney, Australia.

Health & Safety Executive (2013). *Education*, http://www.hse.gov.uk/services/education/index.htm.

Heaton, L. A. & Washington, L. A. (1999). Developing technology training for principals. In *Proceedings of American Educational Research Association* (AERA), Montreal, April, 19–23.

Hemphill, J. & Coons, A. (1957). Development of the leader behavior description questionnaire. In R. Stogdill & A. Coons (eds) *Leader Behavior: Its description and measurement*. Columbus, OH: Bureau for Business Research, Ohio State University.

Hill, D. (2001). Equality, ideology and education policy. In D. Hill & M. Cole, *Schooling and Equality: Fact, concept and policy*. London: Kogan Page.

Hill, D. & Cole, M. (2001). *Schooling and Equality: Fact, concept and policy*. London: Kogan Page.

Hill, R. & Matthews, P. (2010). *Schools Leading Schools II: The growing impact of national leaders of education*. Nottingham: National College for Leadership of Schools and Children's Services.

Hirsh, W. (2010). Positive career development for leaders. In J. Storey (ed.) *Leadership in Organizations: Current issues and key trends*, 2nd edn. London: Routledge.

Holligan, C., Menter, I., Hutchings, M. & Walker, M. (2006). Becoming a headteacher: the perspectives of new headteachers in twenty-first century England, *Journal of In-Service Education*, 32(1), pp. 103–22.

Hope, W. C. & Stakenas, R. G. (1999). Leading the technology revolution: a new challenge for principals. In F. Kochan (ed.) *Southern Regional Conference on Educational Leadership 1999 Yearbook: Leadership for the 21st Century*. Auburn, AL: University of Truman Pierce Institute.

Hosking, D. M. (1988). Organizing, leadership and skilful process, *Journal of Management Studies*, 25, pp. 147–66.

Hughes, J. E. (2013.) Indicators of future teachers' technology integration in the PK-12 classroom: trends from a laptop-infused teacher education program, *Journal of Educational Computing Research*, 48(4), pp. 493–518.

Hughes, M. (1976). The professional-as-administrator: the case of the secondary school head. In R. S. Peters (ed.) *The Role of the Head*. London: Routledge & Kegan Paul.

Hughes, M. (1995). Theory and practice in educational management. In M. Hughes, P. Ribbins and H. Thomas (eds) *Managing Education: The System and the Institution*. London: Holt, Rinehart and Winston.

Hutton, D. (2011). Revealing the essential characteristics, qualities and behaviours of the high performing principal: experiences of the Jamaican school system, *International Journal of Educational Leadership Preparation*, 5(3), pp. 1–15.

International Society for Technology in Education (2008). *Technology and Student Achievement – The indelible link*. Washington, DC: ISTE.

Jennings, R. (1977). *Education and Politics: Policy Making in Local Education Authorities*. London: Batsford.

Johnston, J. & Montecino, J. A. (2012). *Update on the Jamaican Economy*. Washington: Center for Economic and Policy Research.

Jones, A. (1987). *Leadership for Tomorrow's Schools*. Oxford: Blackwell.

Jones, G. & Hayes, D. (1991). Primary headteachers and ERA two years on: the pace of change and its impact upon schools, *School Organisation*, 11(2), pp. 211–21.

Lai, K.W. & Pratt, K. (2004). Information Communication Technology (ICT) in secondary schools: The role of the computer coordinator, *British Journal of Educational Technology*, 35(4), pp. 461–75.

Lawton, S. B. (2010). Designing and using academic information systems. In R. Papa (ed.) *Technology for Educational Leaders*. Thousand Oaks, CA: Sage.

Leachman, M. & Mai, C. (2014). *Most States Funding Schools Less than Before the Recession*. Washington: Center on Budget and Policy Priorities.

Lee, J-W. (1999). *Economic Growth and Human Development in the Republic of Korea: 1945–1992*. New York: United Nations Development Programme.

Leithwood, K. & Jantzi, D. (2008). Linking leadership to student learning: the role of collective efficacy, *Educational Administration Quarterly*, 44(4), pp. 496–528.

Leithwood, K. & Seashore-Louis, K. (2012). *Linking Leadership to Student Learning*. San Francisco: Jossey-Bass.

Leithwood, K., Louis, K., Anderson, S. & Wahlstrom, K. (2004). *How Leadership Influences Student Learning*. New York: Wallace Foundation.

Lewis, P. & Murphy, R. (2008). New directions in school leadership, *School Leadership and Management*, 28(2), pp. 12–46.

Linn, R. & Haug, C. (2002). Stability of school-building accountability scores and gains, *Educational Evaluation and Policy Analysis*, 24, pp. 29–36.

Livingston, A. & Wirt, J. (2005). *The Condition of Education 2005 in Brief* (NCES 2005–095). Washington: US Department of Education/National Center for Education Statistics.

Lubienski, C. (2009). Do quasi-markets foster innovation in education? A comparative perspective, *OECD Education Working Papers* 25. Paris: OECD.

Lucas, R. E. (1993). Making a miracle, *Econometrica*, 61, pp. 251–72.

MacBeath, J. (2008). Leading learning in the self-evaluating school, *School Leadership and Management*, 28(4), pp. 385–99.

MacGilchrist, B. (2003). *Has School Improvement Passed its Sell-by Date?* Professorial Lecture, London: Institute of Education.

Maden, M. & Hillman, J. (1996). *Success Against the Odds*. London: Routledge.

Marzano, R. J., Waters, T. & McNulty, B. A. (2005). *School Leadership that Works: From research to results*. Alexandria, VA: ASCD.

Maslow, A. H. (1950). Social theory of motivation. In M. Shore (ed.) *Twentieth Century Mental Hygiene: New directions in mental health*, pp. 347–57. New York: Social Sciences.

Maslowski, R. (2001). *School Culture and School Performance: An exploratory study into the organizational culture of secondary schools and their effects*. Enschede, the Netherlands: Twente University Press.

Matthews, P., Rea, S., Hill, R. & Gu, Q. (2014). *Freedom to Lead: A study of outstanding primary school leadership in England, research report*. Nottingham: Isos Partnership/NCTL.

McAllister, K. & Hadjri, K. (2013). Inclusion and the special educational needs (SEN) resource base in mainstream schools: physical factors to maximise effectiveness, *Support for Learning*, 28(2), pp. 57–65.

McGregor, D. (1996). *The Human Side of Enterprise: Annotated Edition*. Maidenhead: McGraw-Hill.

McGregor, J. (2000). The challenge of collaboration: what encourages joint work between teachers? Paper presented at BEMAS Research Conference, Cambridge, July.

McHugh, M. & McMullan, L. (1995). Headteacher or manager? Implications for Training and development, *School Organisation*, 15(1), pp. 23–34.

Means, B. & Olson, K. (1995). *Technology's Role in Educational reform: Findings from a national study of innovating schools*, Office of Educational Research and Improvement. Washington: US Department of Education.

Menter, I., Muschamp, Y., Nichols, P., Pollard, P. & Ozga, J. (1995). Still carrying the can: primary school headship in the 1990s, *School Organisation*, 15, pp. 301–12.

Merry, U. (1995). *Coping with Uncertainty: Insights from the new sciences of chaos, self-organisation and complexity.* Westport, CT: Praeger.

Miliband, D. (2003). Challenges for school leadership, speech to the Secondary Heads Association's conference, London, Tuesday 1 July.

Miller, P. (2011). Free schools, free choice and the academisation of education in England, *Research in Comparative International Education*, 6(2), pp. 168–80.

Miller, P. (2012). The changing nature of educational leadership: 'educational leadership in the Caribbean & beyond' (editorial), *Journal of the University College of the Cayman Islands*, Special Issue, JUCCI 6, December.

Miller, P. (ed.) (2013a). *School Leadership in the Caribbean: Perceptions, practices, paradigms.* London: Symposium Books.

Miller, P. (2013b). *The Politics of Progression: Primary teachers' perceived barriers to gaining a principalship in Jamaica.* Research report. Kingston: University of Technology, Jamaica & the Institute for Educational Administration & Leadership Jamaica.

Miller, P. (2013c). Feedback equals feedforward: issues in teacher progression and development among primary teachers in Jamaica, *International Studies in Educational Administration*, 41(3), pp. 19–30.

Miller, P. (2014). Becoming a principal: exploring perceived discriminatory practices in the selection of principals in Jamaica and England. In K. Beycioglu & P. Pashiardis (eds) *Multidimensional Perspectives on Principal Leadership Effectiveness.* Hershey, PA: IGI Publishers.

Miller, P. & Hutton, D. (2014). Leading from 'within': towards a comparative view of how school leaders' personal values and beliefs influence how they lead in England and Jamaica. In S. Harris & J. Mixon (eds) *Building Cultural Community through Global Educational Leadership.* Ypsilanti, MI: NCPEA Publications.

Miller, P. & Potter, I. (2014). Teacher CPD across borders: reflections on how a study tour to England helped to change the practice and praxis among Jamaican teachers, *International Journal of Education and Practice*, 2(1), pp. 9–20.

Mitchell, C. & Sackney, L. (2000). *Profound Improvement: Building capacity for a learning community.* Lisse, NL: Swets & Zeitlinger.

Modood, T. & May, S. (2001). Multiculturalism and education in Britain: an internally contested debate, *International Journal of Educational Research*, 35(3), pp. 305–17.

MoE (Ministry of Education) (2012). *Education Statistics 2011–2012: Annual statistical review of the education sector.* Kingston, Jamaica: Planning and Development Division, MoE.

Mortimore, P. & Mortimore, J. (1991). *The Primary Head: Roles, responsibilities and reflections.* London: Paul Chapman.

Mortimore, P. & Whitty, G. (1997). *Can School Improvement Overcome the Effects of Disadvantage?* London: Institute of Education.

Muijs, D. and Harris, A. (2003). Teacher leadership: improvement through empowerment, *Educational Management and Administration*, 31(4), pp. 437–49.

Nadler, D. & Tushman, M. (1990). Beyond the charismatic leader: leadership and organisational change, *California Management Review*, 23(3), pp. 77–97.

Nance, J. P. (2003). Public school administrators and technology policy making (1 October 2003), *Educational Administration Quarterly*, 39(4), pp. 434–67.

National Education Inspectorate (2010). *Chief Inspector's Report: Inspection cycle, round 2*, November. Kingston: Ministry of Education.

Negus, E. (2014). Lessons for the 21st Century from Victorian utilitarian education, *Education Today*, 64(3), pp.18–24.

Ng, W. (2008). Transformational leadership and the integration of information and communications technology into teaching, *The Asia-Pacific Education Researcher*, 17(1), pp. 1–14.

Nias, J. (1980). Leadership styles and job satisfaction in primary schools. In T. Bush, R. Glatter, J. Goodey & C. Riches (eds) *Approaches to School Management*. London: Harper Row.

Northouse, P. G. (2012). *Leadership: Theory and Practice*. London: Sage.

Ofsted (Office for Standards in Education) (2004). *Special Educational Needs And Disability: Towards inclusive schools*. London: Ofsted.

Ofsted (Office for Standards in Education) (2009). *Twenty Outstanding Primary Schools: Excelling against the odds in challenging circumstances*. London: Ofsted.

Ofsted (Office for Standards in Education) (2012). Press release: the importance of leadership – The Annual Report of Her Majesty's Chief Inspector of Education, Children's Services and Skills 2011/12, ref: NR2012-38. Manchester: Ofsted.

Ofsted (Office for Standards in Education) (2013). *Unseen Children: Access and achievement 20 years on. Evidence report*. Manchester: Ofsted.

Olssen, M., Codd, J. & O'Neill, A. (2004). *Education Policy: Globalization, citizenship and democracy*. London: Sage.

Parker, J. D. A., Hogan, M. J., Eastabrook, J. M., Oke, A. & Wood, L. M. (2006). Emotional intelligence and student retention: predicting the successful transition from high school to university, *Personality and Individual Differences*, 41, pp. 1329–36.

Patrinos, H. A., Ridao-Cano, C. & Sakellariou, C. (2006). *Estimating the Returns to Education: Accounting for heterogeneity*, policy research working paper 4040. Washington, DC: The World Bank.

Peters, T. (2013). *Four Ways to Become a Leader People Want to Follow*, http://michaelhyatt.com/a-leader-people-want-to-follow.html.

Peters, T. & Waterman, R. (1982). *In Search of Excellence: Lessons from America's best run companies*. New York: Harper & Row.

Picketty, T. (2014). *Capital in the 21st Century*, Boston, MA: Harvard University Press.

Pollard, A., Broadfoot, T., Croll, P., Osborn, M. & Abbott, D. (1994). *Changing English Primary Schools? The impact of the Education Reform Act at Key Stage 1*. London: Cassell.

Prensky, M. (2005). Engage me or enrage me: learners demand, *Educause Review*, September/October, pp. 60–4.

Prensky, M. (2010). *Teaching Digital Natives: Partnering for real learning.* London: Corwin.

PricewaterhouseCoopers LLP (2007). *Independent Study into School Leadership*, DfES, research report DfESRR818A. London: HMSO.

Prokopiadou, G. (2012). Using information and communication technologies in school administration: researching Greek kindergarten schools, *Educational Management Administration and Leadership*, 40(3), pp. 305–27.

Psacharopoulos, G. & Patrinos, A. H. (2004). Return to investment in education: a further update, *Education Economics*, 12(2), pp. 112–33.

Race, R. (2013). Reflections on multiculturalism and education, *Contemporary Issues in Education*, 3(10), pp. 7–22.

Race, R. & Lander, V. (eds) (2014). *Advancing Race and Ethnicity in Education.* London: Palgrave Macmillan.

Rayner, S. (2014). Playing by the rules? The professional values of headteachers tested by the changing policy context, *Management in Education*, 28(2), pp. 38–43.

Rayner, S. and Ribbins, P. (1999). *Head Teachers and Leadership in Special Education.* London: Cassell.

Reynolds, D. & Cuttance, P. (1992). *School Effectiveness: Research Policy and Practice.* London: Cassell.

Reynolds, D., Harris, A., Clarke, P., Harris, B. & James, S. (2006). Challenging the challenged: improving schools in exceptionally challenging circumstances, *School Effectiveness and School Improvement*, 17(4), pp. 425–41.

Ribbins, P. (1999). Foreword. In P. T. Begley & P. E. Leonard (eds) *The Values of Educational Administration.* London: Falmer Press.

Ribbins, P. & Marland, M. (1994). *Headship Matters.* Harlow: Longman.

Riley, K. (2013). *Leadership of Place: Stories from the US, UK and South Africa.* London: Bloomsbury.

Riley, K. A. (2000). Leadership, learning and systemic reform, *Journal of Educational Change*, 1(1), pp. 29–55.

Riley, K. A., Dockings, J. & Rowles, D. (2000). Caught between local education authorities: making a difference through their leadership. In K. A. Riley & K. S. Louis (eds) *Leadership for Change and School Reform.* London: RoutledgeFalmer.

Rimmer, J. (2013). *The Four Dimensions of Instructional Leadership: What school leaders must do to improve teaching effectiveness.* Washington: University of Washington Center for Educational Leadership.

Rivera-Batiz, F. L. (2007). *Is Education an Engine of Economic Growth?: Myth and reality.* New York: Program in Economics and Education, Teachers College, Columbia University.

Rivera-Batiz, F. L. (2008). *Education as an Engine of Economic Development: Global experiences and prospects for El Salvador.* Research Monograph prepared for Fundación Salvadoreña para el Desarrollo Económico y Social FUSADES.

Rodgers, C. (2013). *Taking Organisational Complexity Seriously: a White Paper, Centre For Progressive Leadership*. London: London Metropolitan University.

Roomi, M. A. & Harrison, P. (2011). Entrepreneurial leadership: what is it and how should it be taught? *International Review of Entrepreneurship*, 9(3), pp. 1–44.

Rowe, W. G. & Guerrero, L. (2013). *Cases in Leadership*, 3rd edn. Thousand Oak, CA: Sage.

Sage, R. (2014). Education in a capitalist society, *Education Today*, 64(3), pp. 3–10.

Schedlitzki, D. & Edwards, G. (2014). *Studying Leadership: Traditional and Critical Approaches*. London: Sage.

Scheerens, J. (ed.) (2012). *School Leadership Effects Revisited: Review and meta-analysis of empirical studies*. London: Springer.

Schiller, J. (2002). Interventions by school leaders in effective implementation of information and communications technology: perceptions of Australian principals, *Technology, Pedagogy and Education*, 11(3), pp. 289–301.

Schleicher, A. (2012). *Preparing Teachers and Developing School Leaders for the 21st Century*. Paris: OECD.

Schultz, T. W. (1963). *The Economic Value of Education*. New York: Columbia University Press.

Senge, P. (1990). *The Fifth Discipline*. New York: Doubleday.

Senge, P. (2006). *The Fifth Discipline*, 2nd edn. London: Century.

Shah, S. & Shaikh, J. (2010). Leadership progression of Muslim male teachers: interplay of ethnicity, faith and visibility, *School Leadership & Management*, 30(1), pp. 19–33.

Sherrington, T. (2012). Dealing with grief: how schools can offer sanctuary, normality and support, http://www.theguardian.com/teacher-network/teacher-blog/2012/nov/29/grief-in-school-students-support-bereavement.

Shotte, G. (2003). Education, migration and identities among relocated montserratian students in British schools, http://www.open.uwi.edu/sites/default/files/bnccde/montserrat/conference/papers/shotte.html.

Shotte, G. (2013). School leadership for sustainable education: reflections on Montserrat. In P. Miller (ed.) *School Leadership in the Caribbean: Perceptions, practices, paradigms*. London: Symposium Books.

Sikes, P. & Piper, H. (2010). *Researching sex and lies in the classroom: Allegations of sexual misconduct in schools*. London: RoutledgeFalmer.

Simkins, T. (1997). Managing resources. In H. Tomlinson (ed.) *Managing Continual Professional Development in Schools*. London: Paul Chapman.

Smith, E. (2012). *Key Issues in Education and Social Justice*. London: Sage.

Smith, J. (2011). Aspirations to and perceptions of secondary headship: contrasting female teachers' and headteachers' perspectives, *Educational Management Administration and Leadership*, 39(5), pp. 516–35.

Southworth, G. W. (1993). School leadership and school development: reflections from research, *School Organisation*, 13, pp. 73–87.

Southworth, G. W. (1995). Reflections on mentoring for new school leaders, *Journal of Educational Administration*, 33(5), pp. 17–28.

Spillane, J. P. (2006). *Distributed Leadership*. San Francisco: Jossey-Bass.

Starratt, R. J. (1999). Moral dimensions of leadership. In P. T. Begley & P. E. Leonard (eds) *The Values of Educational Administration*. London: Falmer Press.

Stevens, J., Brown, J., Knibbs, S. & Smith, J. (2005). *Follow-up Research into the State of School Leadership in England*. London: DfES.

Stiglitz, J. (2012). *The Price of Inequality*. New York: W. W. Norton & Co.

Stogdill, R. M. (1950). Leadership, membership and organization, *Psychological Bulletin*, 47, pp. 1–14.

Stogdill, R. M. (1974). *Handbook of Leadership: A Survey of the Literature*. New York: Free Press.

Stoker, G. (2006). Public value management: a new narrative for networked governance?, *American Review of Public Administration*, 36(1), pp. 41–57.

Suchman, M. C. (1995). Managing legitimacy: strategic and institutional approaches, *Academy of Management Journal*, 20(3), pp. 571–610.

Tan, S. C. (2010). Technology leadership: lessons from empirical research. In C. H. Steel, M. J. Keppell, P. Gerbic & S. Housego (eds) *Curriculum, Technology & Transformation for an Unknown Future*, Proceedings ascilite, Sydney.

Task Force on Educational Reform (2005). *A Transformed Education System Report* – revised edn. Kingston: Jamaica Information Service.

Taylor, S., Rizvi, F., Lingard, B. & Henry, M. (1997). *Educational Policy and the Politics of Change*. London: Routledge.

Technology Standards for School Administrators Collaborative (2010). www.ncrtec.org/pd/tssa/tssa.pdf.

Thomas, R. & Davies, A. (2005). Theorizing the micro-politics of resistance: new public management and managerial identities in the UK Public services, *Organization Studies*, 26(5), pp. 683–706.

Thomson, P. (2010). Headteacher autonomy: a sketch of Bourdieuian field analysis of position and practice, *Critical Studies in Education*, 51(1), pp. 5–20.

Tomlinson, H. (1997). *Managing Continuing Professional Development in Schools*. London: Paul Chapman.

Tondeur, J., Devos, G., Van Houtte, M., Van Braak, J. & Valcke, M. (2009). Understanding structural and cultural school characteristics in relation to educational change: the case of ICT integration, *Educational Studies*, 35(2), pp. 223–35.

Torrington, D. & Weightman, J. (1989). *The Reality of School Management*. Oxford: Basil Blackwell.

Townsend, T. & MacBeath, J. (2011). Leadership for learning: paradoxes, paradigms and principles. In T. Townsend and J. MacBeath (eds) *International Handbook of Leadership for Learning*. Rotterdam: Springer.

Triandafyllidou, A., Modood, T. & Meer, T. (2012). Introduction: diversity, integration, secularism, and multiculturalism. In A. Triandafyllidou, T. Modood and T. Meer (eds) *European Multiculturalisms: Cultural, Religious and ethnic challenges*. Edinburgh: Edinburgh University Press.

Troyna, B. & Hatcher, R. (1992). *Racism in Children's Lives: A study of mainly-white primary schools*. London: Routledge.

Tyack, D. & Cuban, L. (1995). *Tinkering Toward Utopia: A century of public school reform*. Cambridge, MA: Harvard University Press.

Ullman, E. (2013). Technology and Education Reform, http://www.k12blueprint.com/content/technology-and-education-reform.

UNESCO (1960). *Convention Against Discrimination in Education*, 14 December, http://www.refworld.org/docid/3ae6b3880.html.

UNESCO (1995). *Multiculturalism: A policy response to diversity*, http://www.unesco.org/most/sydpaper.htm.

UNICEF (2005). *Gender Achievements and Prospects in Education: The Gap Report*. New York: UNICEF.

UNICEF/Innocenti Research Centre (2004). *Ensuring the Rights of Indigenous Children*, Innocenti Digest no. 11. Florence.

United Nations (1989). *Convention on the Rights of the Child*, 20 November, http://www.refworld.org/docid/3ae6b38f0.html.

United Nations. (2010). *The Millennium Development Goals Report 2010*. New York: United Nations.

United Nations (2011). *The right to education of migrants, refugees and asylum seekers: report of the Special Rapporteur on the right to education*, A/HRC/14/25. New York: UN General Assembly.

United Nations (2013). *The Millennium Development Goals Report 2013*. New York: United Nations.

US Congress, Senate Committee on Equal Educational Opportunity (1970). *Toward Equal Educational Opportunity*. Washington, DC: Government Printing Office.

van Engen, M. L., van der Leeden, R. & Willemsen, T. M. (2001). Gender, context, and leadership styles: a field study, *Journal of Occupational and Organizational Psychology*, 74, pp. 581–98.

van Velzen, W., Miles., Ekholm, M., Hameyer, U. & Robin, D. (1985). *Making School Improvement Work: A conceptual guide to practice*. Leuven, Belgium: Acco.

Warschauer, M., Knobel, M. & Stone, L. (2004). Technology and equity in schooling: deconstructing the digital divide, *Educational Policy*, 18(4), pp. 562–88.

Wasserberg, M. (1999). Creating the vision and making it happen, in H. Tomlinson, H. Gunter & P. Smith (eds) *Living Headship: Voices, Values and Vision*. London: Paul Chapman.

Watson, P. (2013). Every click matters: leadership and followership in ICT education in Jamaica. In P. Miller (ed.) *School Leadership in the Caribbean: Perceptions, practices, paradigms*. London: Symposium Books.

Webb, R. & Vulliamy, G. J. (1996). A deluge of directives: conflict between collegiality and managerialism in the post-ERA primary school, *British Educational Research Journal*, 22(4), pp. 441–58.

WEF (World Economic Forum) (2014). *The Global Gender Gap Report 2014*. Geneva: WEF, http://www3.weforum.org/docs/GGGR14/GGGR_CompleteReport_2014. pdf.

Wenger, E. (1991). Communities of practice: the key to a knowledge strategy, *Knowledge Directions*, 1(2), pp. 48–63.

West, M., Jackson, D., Harris, A. and Hopkins, D. (2000). Leadership for school improvement, in K. Riley and K. Seashore-Louis, *Leadership for Change*. London: Routledge/Falmer Press.

Whitehead, B. M., Jensen, F. N. D. & Boschee, F. (2003). *Planning for Technology: A guide for school administrators, technology coordinators, and curriculum leaders*. Thousand Oaks, CA: Corwin.

Whitehead, J. (1985). An analysis of an individual's educational development – the basis for personally orientated action research, in M. Shipman (ed.) *Educational Research: Principles, Policies and Practice*. London: Falmer.

Whitty, G. & Anders, J. (2012). (How) did New Labour narrow the achievement and participation gap? Paper presented at a seminar of the Centre for Learning and Life Chances in Knowledge Economies and Societies (LLAKES), Institute of Education, University of London, 5 December.

Wilkin, A., Derrington, C., White, R., Martin, K., Foster, B., Kinder, K. & Rutt, S. (2010). Improving the outcomes for Gypsy, Roma and Traveller pupils: final report (Ref: DFE-RR043). Slough: National Foundation for Educational Research.

Wilkinson, R. & Picket, K. (2009). *The Spirit Level: Why more equal societies almost always do better*. London: Penguin Books.

Woolf, A. (2000). *Does Education Matter? Myths about education and economic growth*. London: Penguin.

World Bank (1995). *Constructing Knowledge Societies: New challenges for tertiary education*. Washington, DC: The World Bank.

Wright, H., Sing, M. & Race, R. (2012). Multiculturalism and multicultural education: precarious hegemonic, status quo and alternatives. In W. Handel, M. Singh & R. Race (eds) *Precarious International Multicultural Education: Hegemony, dissent and rising alternatives*. Rotterdam: Sense Publishers.

Yee, D. L. (2000). Images of school principals' information and communications technology leadership, *Technology, Pedagogy and Education*, 9(3), pp. 287–302.

Yuen, A., Law, N. & Wong, K. (2003). ICT implementation and school leadership, *Journal of Educational Administration*, 41(2), pp. 158–70.

Yukl, G. (2012). *Leadership in Organizations*, 8th edn. Upper Saddle River, NJ: Pearson/ Prentice Hall.

Index